D0915160

THE LIVING WORD COMMENTARY

Editor
Everett Ferguson

The Gospel
According to Mark

The Gospel
According to Mark

Earle McMillan

SWEET PUBLISHING COMPANY

Austin, Texas

LIBRARY OF CONGRESS CATALOG CARD NUMBER: 72-86991

STANDARD BOOK NUMBER: 8344-0066-9

PRINTED IN U.S.A.

Acknowledgment

This commentary is based on the text of the Revised Standard
Version of the Bible, copyrighted 1946, 1952 and 1971 by the
Division of Christian Education, National Council of the
Churches of Christ in the U.S.A., and used by permission.

Writers in *The Living Word Commentary* series have been
given freedom to develop their own understanding of the biblical text. As long as a fair statement is given to alternative in-
terpretations, each writer has been permitted to state his own
conclusions. Beyond the general editorial policies, the editors
have sought no artificial uniformity, and differences are
allowed free expression. A writer is responsible for his con-
tribution alone, and the views expressed are not necessarily
the views of the editors or publisher.

Contents

I. INTRODUCTION   7
   Background   7
   Analysis   9
   Sonship, Messianic Secret   13
   Miscellaneous   15
      Chronology and Geography   15
      Vividness   16
      Synoptic Problem   17
   Selected Bibliography   18
      Commentaries   18
      Special Studies   18

II. THE GOSPEL ACCORDING TO MARK   19
   The Beginning of the Gospel, 1:1-13   19
   The Galilean Ministry, 1:14—8:26   25
   The Way to Jerusalem, 8:27—10:52   101
   Jerusalem-Judean Ministry, 11:1—12:44   133
   The Markan Apocalypse, 13:1-37   155
   The Passion Narrative, 14:1—16:8   164
   Epilogue, 16:9-20   190

I

Introduction

BACKGROUND

The word gospel, meaning "good news," was first used in reference to the good news about Christ in the preaching of the earliest church. Once the earliest oral preaching was put in written form the term quickly adapted itself to the new situation and at least from the time of Justin (*circa* A. D. 150) was used of the written form of the message.

The preaching of the early church was not put in the form of written gospels until the eyewitnesses began to pass from the scene. Then, sometime after that, there began to arise an interest in the origin, nature, and characteristics of these written sources of the life of Jesus, as well as those documents which gave an insight into the way in which the early church should conduct itself. In all of this the primary concern seems to have been with *apostolic* witness.

Papias, who was bishop of Hierapolis (near Colossae) about A. D. 140, and as far as is known the first to comment specifically on Mark's Gospel, said:

> This also the Elder said: Mark, who became Peter's interpreter, wrote accurately, though not in order, all that he remembered of the things said or done by the Lord. For he had neither heard the Lord nor been one of his followers, but afterwards, as I said, he had followed Peter, who used to compose his discourses with a view to the needs [of his hearers], but not as if he were composing a systematic account of the Lord's sayings. So Mark did nothing blameworthy in thus writing some things just as he remembered them; for he was careful of this one thing, to omit none of the things he had heard and to make no untrue statement therein. (Eusebius, *Church History III.39*)

7

INTRODUCTION

Some twenty to forty years later, an unknown Christian writer, writing against Marcion, an early heretic, wrote:

> . . . Mark declared, who is called "Stump-fingered" because he had short fingers in comparison with the rest of his body. He was Peter's interpreter. After the death of Peter himself he wrote down this same gospel in the regions of Italy. *(Anti-Marcionite Prologue to Mark)*

Irenaeus, about A.D. 180 affirmed:

> And after their [i.e., Peter's and Paul's] deaths Mark, the disciple and interpreter of Peter, himself also handed down to us in writing the things preached by Peter. *(Against Heresies III.i.1)*

This is the second-century tradition concerning the gospel of Mark. Not only is it self-consistent, but it establishes a number of significant points. First, Mark is clearly set forth as the author of the Gospel bearing his name. This is important, for nowhere in the Gospel itself does Mark claim to have written the document. Through Mark's association with Peter (see 1 Peter 5:13), the importance of apostolic witness mentioned earlier is underlined. That Mark was Peter's "interpreter" *(hermeneutēs)* is supported by all three authors and seems to suggest something like "personal secretary." That is, it suggests a relationship of some depth and importance to the men concerned. Next, the testimony of the Anti-Marcionite writer establishes Italy as the place of writing. This would explain certain things that may be observed in the Gospel: the use of transliterated Latin terms *(centurio,denarius,* etc.), the careful translation of Aramaic expressions *(Talitha cumi,* 5:41; *Ephphatha,* 7:34), and the explanation of Jewish customs (7:3f.; 14:12; and 15:42; etc.). And finally, there seems to be clear witness to the fact that Mark's Gospel was not arranged in strict chronological order but rather followed those lines established in Peter's preaching, which was ordered on the basis of the needs of his audience. All of these points will become increasingly important as one examines both the Gospel itself and the insights provided by scripture into the situation that produced the Gospel.

The later tradition concerning Mark and his Gospel seems, in the main, to be confirmed by the biblical evidence. Although Mark, the cousin of Barnabas (Col. 4:10), began his service in the development of the church with some difficulty (Acts 13:13 and 15:36-41), he later established himself as a dependable man both with Peter (1 Peter 5:13) and Paul (2 Tim. 4:11). This last reference, if the desire were realized, would put Mark in Rome just about the time suggested by the Anti-Marcionite writer. The traditional date assigned to the Gospel has been A. D. 65-70, i.e., sometime near the death of Peter (and Paul?, see above) and before the destruction of Jerusalem (anticipated in chapter 13).

Mark's mother was influential in the church at Jerusalem (Acts 12:12ff.), and it has therefore been tempting to many commentators to speculate that the "upper room" where the apostles stayed between the ascension and Pentecost (Acts 1:13) was a part of Mary's house. If this is true—and it is only a possibility—it is an easy step to link that upper room with the upper room of the last supper. This would make it conceivable that the young man who followed Jesus the night of the betrayal with only a cloth wrapped around his body (14:51f.) was none other than the evangelist himself. Some corroboration for such a view is found in the fact that this incident is not mentioned in any of the other Gospels (see comments on 14:51f.). In any case, it is clear that Mark was himself reasonably close to the historical Jesus, although not a part of the inner circle of disciples.

ANALYSIS

While there has been general agreement that Mark represents the first of the written Gospels, there has not been as wide an agreement as to precisely how Mark himself conceived his literary purpose. Some have argued that there was no purpose, that if anything like purpose might be observed (comparisons are possible between the Gospel and Peter's sermon to Cornelius in Acts 10) it should be reckoned as a residue from Peter's preaching. While this must be taken into account, it should not be considered the whole story.

It is quite likely that the first thing to have been written about the life of Jesus was a passion narrative. This would have been mainly for devotional purposes at the worship services of the early church. In this connection, it should be noted that some two-fifths of Mark concerns the last few days of Jesus' life. Some have therefore analyzed Mark as a passion narrative with an extended introduction. While this may be true, in some sense it does an injustice to Mark's literary prowess.

The primary question in Mark has to do with the identity of the central figure. The central point of view expressed in this commentary is that the Gospel is specifically concerned to lead the reader indirectly to the conclusion that Jesus is the Anointed One of God. The same may well have been true of Peter's preaching. It should be kept in mind that Peter's purpose in preaching may have been the same as Mark's in writing. From a literary point of view, even the crucifixion plays a role dependent upon Jesus' identity. The importance of this point should perhaps be obvious. If Jesus were not the Christ, then his death is relatively insignificant. This point cannot be overstressed. It is for this reason that those whom Jesus encountered in the Gospel reacted so deeply in questions like, "What is this?" (1:27), or exclamations such as, "We never saw anything like this!" (2:12). The classic form of the issue is found at the end of the story of the stilling of the storm, "Who then is this, that even wind and sea obey him?" (4:41). This is precisely the question that Mark intended to raise with the entire Gospel.

It is possible to show that Mark intended that his reader come to the same conclusion—as the result of perusing the same evidence—that Peter himself came to when Jesus put the question to him, "But who do you say that I am?" It is in this way that Peter's confession becomes the pivot of the entire Markan narrative. An examination of the distribution and development of certain central themes will settle this beyond any reasonable doubt.

Nowhere does this fundamental purpose of establishing Jesus' identity appear more clearly than it does in the narratives concerning Jesus' miracles (a distinction is here made between miracles which Jesus performed and those of which he is the object). Mark records twenty such narratives. They are:

1:21ff. Synagogue Demoniac	4:35ff. Stilling of the Storm
1:29ff. Peter's Mother-in-law	5:1 ff. Gerasene Demoniac
1:32ff. General Healing	5:21ff. Jairus' Daughter
1:40ff. A Leper	5:25ff. Woman with Hemorrhage
2:1 ff. A Paralytic	6:30ff. Feeding of the Five Thousand
3:1 ff. Man with a Withered Hand	6:45ff. Walking on Water

6:53ff. General Healing	8:22ff. Blind Man of Bethsaida
7:24ff. Demon-possessed Child	9:14ff. An Epileptic Boy
7:31ff. A Deaf Man	10:46ff. Blind Bartimaeus
8:1 ff. Feeding of Four Thousand	11:12ff. Cursing the Fig Tree

The distribution is important. The fact that seventeen of these twenty stories appear in the text prior to Peter's confession (8:27-30) should call attention to itself. The primary emphasis of the first half of the Gospel is placed upon Jesus' expressions of miraculous power. From this standpoint it is not out of order to describe Mark as "the Gospel of Jesus' deeds."

Mark's primary literary purpose in so structuring his narrative of the life of Jesus was to provoke the question of identity: "Who then is this, that even the wind and sea obey him?" (4:41). After Jesus' identity was established (in the Gospel) there was little need for any continued reiteration of his miraculous work. In fact, even in those three miracle stories appearing after Peter's confession, there seems to be a reorientation resulting in a decided emphasis upon faith.

The fact that Mark sensed the importance of Jesus' identity is further illustrated in the development of the concept of suffering. It is significant that in Mark, Jesus himself does not mention suffering until after the confession. This fact alone would seem to confirm the contention that has already been stated, i.e., that it is not important that Jesus died the death he did until it is understood who he was. A resumé of the passages dealing with suffering will help the understanding of the situation.

8:31 And he began to teach them that the Son of man must suffer many things, and be rejected by the elders and the chief priests and the scribes, and be killed, and after three days rise again.

9:9 And as they were coming down the mountain he charged them to tell no one what they had seen, until the Son of man should have risen from the dead.

9:11f. And they asked him, "Why do the scribes say that first Elijah must come?" And he said to them, "Elijah does come first to restore all things; and how is it written of the Son of man, that he should suffer many things and be treated with contempt?

9:31 For he was teaching his disciples, saying to them, "The Son of man will be delivered into the hands of men, and they will kill him; and when he is killed, after three days he will rise."

11

10:32ff.   And taking the twelve again, he began to tell them what was to happen to him, saying, "Behold, we are going up to Jerusalem; and the Son of man will be delivered to the chief priests and the scribes, and they will condemn him to death, and deliver him to the Gentiles; and they will mock him, and spit upon him, and scourge him, and kill him; and after three days he will rise."

10:45   For the Son of man also came not to be served but to serve, and to give his life as a ransom for many.

14:21   For the Son of man goes as it is written of him, but woe to that man by whom the Son of man is betrayed! It would have been better for that man if he had not been born."

14:41f.   And he came the third time, and said to them, "Are you still sleeping and taking your rest? It is enough; the hour has come; the Son of man is betrayed into the hands of sinners. Rise, let us be going; see, my betrayer is at hand."

Of the eight open statements that Jesus made about his suffering, six appear between Peter's confession and the beginning of the events which led to crucifixion. There is no open mention of suffering prior to the confession. Again, the very placing of these sayings is significant and contributes to the understanding of Mark's objective in writing his Gospel.

The first statement of Jesus regarding his suffering occurs immediately after the confession. This fact further stresses the importance of the structure of the Gospel. Jesus literally "began" at that point to speak of rejection and ultimate death. Prior to this specific point, this discussion would have been out of place. Again, one is forced to conclude that it was only because Jesus was the Son of God that he could offer himself for sin. The sacrifice of no other would have been effective.

The last two statements concerning suffering, if viewed in context, seem to serve as links between the earlier, more predictive statements and the actual involvement of Jesus in things which led to his death. This is to imply also that the eight passages listed are not absolutely inclusive. That is, there are other inferences and allusions to Jesus' suffering, particularly in the later chapters of the Gospel. These eight sayings are, however, the only places where Jesus discussed the matter during his ministry. The other incidents are largely concerned with the development of the actual suffering situation.

The fact that the first discussion of suffering occurs immediately after the confession is in itself significant. Yet when this is linked to the earlier provocative purpose of Jesus' miracles, the case would seem to be conclusive.

SONSHIP, MESSIANIC SECRET

If Mark reiterates the miracles of Jesus in such a way as to press the question of Jesus' identity, and if suffering is discussed in the Gospel on that basis, and if Peter's realization is seen as the turning point of extreme significance, it might be asked: Just how does the concept of messiahship, sonship, or messianic sonship appear in the Gospel? Although one is sometimes tempted to read implications of one sort or another into other passages (see 1:7; 2:19; and 6:2), the basic statements concerning Jesus' sonship include: 1:1, 11, 24; 2:7; 3:11; 5:7.

The phrase "the Son of God" (1:1) is textually questionable (see comments) and should probably be omitted. The confirmation "from heaven" (1:11) should be understood primarily as a sort of divine approval, a suggestion from the highest authority, the full significance of which was only understood later. The question of the scribes (2:7) is negatively oriented (see comments) and, although putting the suggestion "in the air," cannot be considered anything like a final statement within the structure of the Gospel. This leaves the declarations of the demons (1:24; 3:11; 5:7).

Although some students of the Gospels understand the demons in pyschic terms (sometimes with physical associations), Mark understood them as real representations of the Satanic power. From this point of view their statements with regard to Jesus may be understood as expressions from the "devils" of their own conviction (James 2:19). However the demon narratives may be explained, they must be seen in the Gospel as representing Jesus' (and later his disciples') ultimate triumph over the forces of evil (see 6:7, 13). From this point of view it seems somehow curiously fitting that the first "confessions" of Jesus' identity came from this source. If this is in any way a fair representation of the situation, why then did Jesus charge them to silence (1:25, 34 and 3:12; however, see 5:19)? Indeed, why was there a general charge to silence (see also 1:44; 5:43; 7:36; and

9:9)? This question, that of the "Messianic Secret," has been the object of considerable attention.

German scholarship, led by Wrede, has argued that the charges to silence were insertions by Mark, generated by the fact that although Jesus was the Messiah, he had not been so recognized during his ministry. Mark, knowing that Jesus was the Messiah, felt that he should explain why the Jews did not accept Jesus during his ministry. The answer Mark offered is the "Messianic Secret": Jesus' messiahship was kept secret. It is therefore to be understood as a literary device of Mark and does not reflect the actual situation in the ministry of Jesus. The British view, more broadly based, has been that Jesus enjoined silence because of possible misunderstandings, both nationalistic and otherwise. He did not want his identity declared until he made the character of his mission clear. Questions can of course be raised about both points of view.

There is always the question—as has been indicated—of whether one is dealing with the form of early Christian preaching (Mark or Peter) or Jesus' own self-projection, or indeed both. The view of this commentary tends toward the latter, based in part on assumptions about the nature of the gospel material. In any case, no single suggestion will give adequate reason for every charge to silence. It is a complex issue at best, but the following are suggested as possibilities to be considered: any one or possible combination may apply in a given circumstance. (1) **Nature of the revelation.** It seems quite clear that Jesus revealed himself with great care. He seems to have been more concerned to provoke questions about his identity than openly to declare it. (2) **Timing.** The timing of the revelation must have been important; it could not have been allowed to fall under the well-meaning but inadequately understood ideas of others. (3) **Misunderstandings.** On the one hand there was the problem of religious misunderstanding on the part of the Jews which might have led to significant complications, and, on the other hand, there was always the possibility that the Romans would create difficulty because they understood Jesus to represent a political threat (see comments on 15:2). (4) **Personal or individual situation.** There may have been some reason embedded in the personality of a given individual that resulted in the charge to silence. In this connection it might be noticed that the Gerasene demoniac was told to go and tell. This singular reverse may have been because the Gerasene was a Gentile (see comments). (5) **Situation.** The total collective situation, audience, atmosphere, etc., could have been the occasion for the command to silence. (6) **Jesus' need.** Finally, there were times when Jesus seems to have needed a rest. This could have been at least a part of the reason for a particular charge.

Whatever the nature of the situation, individual or collective, the question of the Messianic Secret must remain something of an enigma. If, however, one sees the role of the demons and the ultimate triumph of Jesus over the forces of Satan as of particular importance, one is compelled to observe that the central issue in both cases was whether or not Jesus was the Son of God. (For a recent discussion of this issue with references, see the article by R. Barbour listed in the bibliography.)

Two further notes should be made at this point: (1) The way in which the usage of the expression "Son of man" enters Mark's purpose is discussed in the comments on 2:28. (2) The nature and purpose of the parables of the kingdom is examined in connection with the comments on chapter four.

MISCELLANEOUS

Chronology and Geography

Mark is at least broadly constructed in historical sequence. Although there is no birth or infancy narrative, the Gospel begins with the ministry of John and the baptism and temptation of Jesus, which is followed by an account of Jesus' ministry. It is concluded with an account of the passion and resurrection. Very early Papias suggested that the incidents recorded of Jesus' ministry were not placed in strict chronological order but rather in a "preaching order," that of Peter, with the best interests of his audience in mind. This seems to be confirmed by the internal evidence: (1) overall distribution of miracle narratives mentioned earlier; (2) closely integrated collections of narratives of a certain type—healing (1:21—2:12), conflict (2:1—3:6); (3)

15

INTRODUCTION

apparent loss of purpose (6:48) or destination (8:10, 22) within a given narrative.

It would therefore appear that strict chronology or consistent reference to geographical location were simply outside Mark's purpose. He had his readers in mind, and all else was put in subjection to this. There is, however, a basic story. It consists of so many trips across Galilee, side trips to Phoenicia and Decapolis, climaxed by one trip to Jerusalem.

Vividness

Any introduction to Mark must include a look at the vividness embedded in the style of the book. Mark is generally thought to have been the first Gospel written. Such a statement represents a broad assumption—one with which we sympathize—which there is simply not enough space here to discuss in detail. One of the reasons for such a conclusion is that although the complete Gospel is shorter than either Matthew or Luke, individual stories—when it is possible to compare them—are usually longer (e.g., examine chapter 5 in a synopsis of the Gospels where the length of the narratives may be compared). The thing that usually makes Mark's account of a given incident longer is attention to detail that regularly leaves a vivid impression of the nature and circumstances of the situation being described.

Examples of this kind of thing may be seen in a number of ways: (1) the occasional inclusion of Aramaic expressions (e.g., 5:11; 7:34, see above); (2) Mark's characteristic use of "immediately" (*euthus*), over forty times in the Gospel; and (3) an emphasis on the impressiveness of Jesus' works and teaching in the use of such words as "fear" (see 4:40; 5:33; 9:6; 10:32; 16:8) and "amazement" (see 6:51; 7:37; 9:15; 10:24, 32; 11:18; 16:5, 6).

While it is valid to make observations such as those just noted, and while it could be argued that those pecularities fit well with Mark's literary purpose, nowhere can one see Mark's vividness better than in an individual story, such as the stilling of the storm (4:35ff.). All of the phrases noted below are found in Mark and in neither of the parallel accounts (Matt. 8:18, 23-27; Luke 8:22-25). They are placed in the form of a list for effect.

16

"when evening had come"	"waves beat into the boat"
"leaving the crowd"	"in the stern"
"they took him with them"	"on the cushion"
"just as he was"	"do you not care"
"other boats were with him"	"peace! Be still"

Anyone familiar with the New Testament has only to glance down the list and the entire incident comes to mind. In fact, the wonder may not be so much that Mark includes such detail but that Matthew and Luke both found it possible to tell the story without using any of these phrases·

Synoptic Problem

The problem concerns both the similarities and the differences that may be observed in the first three Gospels. At points they are very much alike, enough so to compel most who reflect on the question to conclude that there must have been some type of interdependence. At the same time, there are extensive differences. Each Gospel clearly possesses its own character. The question therefore is: how did these two extremely divergent qualities come to exist in the way that they do?

The most popular view is that Mark was the first of the Synoptic Gospels to have been written. And whereas Matthew and Luke were aware of Mark, they were also aware of many other things about Jesus that they felt should be recorded. In fact, it was these other things that made them feel additional Gospels should be written (see Luke 1:1-4). This extra material may have been taken from "sayings" of Jesus then in circulation as well as from the personal experiences of the writers themselves. This kind of an attitude should not be taken as discrediting the concept of inspiration. It may, in fact, represent an attempt to define inspiration more precisely, at least insofar as it demonstrates how humanity was involved in the process of recording the life of Jesus.

INTRODUCTION

SELECTED BIBLIOGRAPHY

Commentaries

CRANFIELD, CHARLES E. *The Gospel According to St. Mark.* Cambridge: Cambridge University Press, 1959.

HUNTER, ARCHIBALD M. *The Gospel According to St. Mark.* New York: Collier Books, 1962.

MOULE, C. F. D. *The Gospel According to Mark.* Cambridge: Cambridge University Press, 1965.

NINEHAM, DENNIS ERIC. *The Gospel of St. Mark.* Baltimore: Penguin Books, 1964.

SCHWEIZER, EDUARD. *The Good News According to Mark.* Trans. Donald Madvig. Richmond: John Knox Press, 1970.

TAYLOR, VINCENT. *The Gospel According to St. Mark.* London: Macmillan, 1952.

Special Studies

BARBOUR, ROBIN S. "Recent Study of the Gospel According to Mark," *Expository Times,* 79 (1968) 324ff.

BEASLEY-MURRAY, GEORGE R. *Jesus and the Future.* London: Macmillan, 1954.

_____. *A Commentary on Mark Thirteen.* London: Macmillan, 1957.

BROWN, R. EDWARD. *Jesus, God and Man.* London: G. Chapman, 1958.

KNOX, JOHN. *The Humanity and Divinity of Christ.* Cambridge: Cambridge University Press, 1967.

LIGHTFOOT, R. H. *The Gospel Message of St. Mark.* New York: Oxford University Press, 1950.

MARXSEN, WILLI. *Mark the Evangelist.* Trans. Roy A. Harrisville. Nashville: Abingdon, 1969.

TURNER, NIGEL. *Grammatical Insights into the New Testament.* Edinburgh: T & T Clark, 1966.

II

The Gospel According to Mark

THE BEGINNING OF THE GOSPEL, 1:1-13

John the Baptist, 1:1-8 (Matt. 3:1-12; Luke 3:1-20; John 1:6, 15, 19-28)

[1] The opening verse of Mark consists of a complete summary of his intention. The reference to **beginning** may recall Genesis 1:1, although in the New Testament it also possesses an almost technical quality when referring to the inauguration of the ministry (see Matt. 4:17; Luke 3:23; Acts 1:1; cf. 10:37). The "good news" is of **Jesus Christ,** and this individual is identified simply, yet profoundly, as **the Son of God.** As noted, some texts omit the phrase **Son of God** which, as will be apparent, would make the development of the theme of sonship much more dramatic.

[2] Mark continues with a citation of Isaiah 40:3. Difficulty lies in the fact that the first part of the quotation does not come from Isaiah but from Malachi 3:1. The solution to this problem may lie in the association of key words. In this case the word **prepare** is found in both Old Testament

¹ **The beginning of the gospel of Jesus Christ, the Son of God.**ᵃ

² **As it is written in Isaiah the prophet,**ᵇ
"Behold I send my messenger before thy face,
who shall prepare thy way;
³ **the voice of one crying in the wilderness:**
Prepare the way of the Lord,
make his paths straight—"
⁴ **John the baptizer appeared**ᶜ **in the wilderness, preaching a baptism of repentance for the forgiveness of sins.** ⁵ **And there went out to him all the country of Judea, and all the people of Jerusalem; and they were baptized by him in the river Jordan, confessing their sins.** ⁶ **Now John was clothed with camel's hair, and had a leather girdle around his waist, and ate locusts and wild honey.**

ᵃ Other ancient authorities omit *the Son of God*
ᵇ Other ancient authorities read *in the prophets*
ᶜ Other ancient authorities read *John was baptizing*

---

quotations and would have tended to draw the two passages together in the author's mind. There is evidence that Jewish writers, followed by the early Fathers, linked scriptures together by associations of this sort. The textual tradition indicates that when the inconsistency was realized, many scribes omitted the reference to Isaiah. In any case, the application of the passage to John the Baptist is an apt one. John is cast in the role of a messenger going in advance of the Messiah and preparing his way. There was the expectation of a return by Elijah (Mal. 4:6) at this time (cf. *Sirach* 48:10 and see notes on Mark 9:11-13).

[3-6] One penetrating figure applied to John is that he was the voice of one crying in the wilderness (Isa. 40:3). John's voice was one of hope in the midst of physical as well as spiritual desolation. His unusual attire and diet, as well as his preaching, attracted the attention of the people. The life that he lived in the desert was not altogether unlike that of the Covenanters (Essenes?) at Qumran (see Vol. 1, pp. 73ff.). Various suggestions have been made to the effect that John was more than casually related to this movement. In fact, the statement of Isaiah 40:3 was taken literally by these people, and they attempted in their way to prepare in the desert the way of the Lord.

⁷ And he preached, saying, "After me comes he who is mightier than I, the thong of whose sandals I am not worthy to stoop down and untie. ⁸ I have baptized you with water; but he will baptize you with the Holy Spirit."

It was there, in relative desolation, that John preached a **baptism of repentance** which resulted in the **forgiveness of sins.** This baptism of John was a preparation for judgment (Matt. 3:11f.; cf. 21:32). Indeed, it was indicative that the person being baptized had accepted the righteousness of God's judgments, especially of the end-time (Luke 7:29f.). There can be no reasonable doubt therefore that John's baptism was considered to be completely preparatory.

John's preaching attracted wide attention (vs. 5). It was in fact directed to "all the people of Israel" (Acts 13:24). There were times, of course, in Israel's past when such repentance was understood to be the only way to avoid national disaster (see e.g., Jer. 3:11-14) and came, as a result, to play a part ultimately in Jewish thinking about the future. In any case, once John aroused the need in his hearers, he challenged them to receive baptism in the river Jordan. Often, early Christian preaching began the story of the gospel with a discussion of the activity of John (Acts 10:37; 13:24; cf. 1:22).

[7, 8] John's message was climaxed by the announcement that there would be another after him **mightier** than he. John felt this man's superiority so much that he suggested that he was not even worthy to unloose his **sandals.** John's feeling in the passage under discussion is made meaningful when it is understood that at the time of Jesus the student owed his teacher everything that a slave owed his master, with the exception of a few menial tasks which included untying sandals. This **mightier** one, John said, would **baptize with the Holy Spirit.** There was a certain association in Jewish thought between the Spirit and power (see Micah 3:8). These terms were used of John himself in comparison with Elijah (Luke 1:17). The same power is, of course, associated with Jesus (Luke 4:14). The kingdom would appear when this power was made available (9:1). John, the prophetic forerunner, only prepared the way for the kingdom. He foresaw that his own baptism

21

⁹ In those days Jesus came from Nazareth of Galilee and was baptized by John in the Jordan. ¹⁰ And when he came up out of the water, immediately he saw the heavens opened and the Spirit descending upon him like a dove; ¹¹ and a voice came from heaven, "Thou art my beloved Son;ᵈ with thee I am well pleased."

ᵈ Or *my Son, my* (or *the*) *Beloved*

---

with water would be followed with a baptism of **the Holy Spirit.**

Jesus' Baptism, 1:9-11 (Matt. 3:13-17; Luke 3:21, 22; John 1:29-34)

[9-11] Marks's statement concerning Jesus' baptism is extremely brief. This may be simply because he was much more concerned with Jesus' deeds. The primary point of concentration is upon the descent of the **Spirit like a dove** and the ensuing blessing from the Father. The account in Mark is manifestly for the purpose of establishing in the reader's mind that Jesus did possess the Spirit and that this fact constituted the approval of the Father. With the exception of 1:1, which is questionable to some extent from a textual point of view, the fact of sonship is found prior to Peter's confession only here and in the narratives concerning the unclean spirits (cf. 1:24; 3:11; 5:7). The language recalls several Old Testament statements (Ps. 2:7; Isa. 42:1; 62:4; Gen. 22:2).

Jesus' acceptance of—indeed, insistence upon—baptism should be understood as Jesus' own approval of God's plan, the righteousness and finality of God's judgment. More personally, it was the designation of Jesus as God's Son. This is established by the use of Psalm 2, which was originally an enthronement Psalm. As royal **Son,** Jesus was anointed with the **Spirit** (Acts 10:38). The personal character of the incident is emphasized by the fact that the statement was made to Jesus alone. The implication is that the story came into the Gospel by some other means than that the disciples were eyewitnesses of the event.

This brings up the question of the "Messianic Secret" which has occupied scholars in this area for many years (see Introduction). The principal issue here is to attempt

¹² **The Spirit immediately drove him out into the wilderness.**
¹³ **And he was in the wilderness forty days, tempted by Satan;
and he was with the wild beasts; and the angels ministered
to him.**

---

some explanation as to why Mark approached the question
of sonship in the way that he did. Mark's allusiveness is
probably based upon the conviction that the sonship of Jesus
could be best apprehended by observing the wonderful things
that Jesus did. That is, every person who confesses Jesus
to be the Son of God must realize Jesus' identity anew
for himself, and this comes primarily in response to a knowledge of what Jesus did. If it can be agreed that Mark reflects
the "gospel preached by Peter," what one finds in the Gospel as a whole, in spite of certain specific references to
bewilderment on the part of some (e.g., 1:27; 2:12), is an
account of Peter's coming to faith in Jesus as the Christ,
the Son of God. It is reasonable to conclude that Mark
hoped his reader would identify with Peter's experience,
especially with regard to the central confession (8:27ff.).
If this is true it, among other things, offers a logical reason
for Mark's deep interest in the deeds of Jesus. It would
also offer an explanation for the fact that interest in Jesus'
deeds, as such, declines after Peter's confession—the long-
sought recognition—and that interest begins at that point
to rise in the suffering and approaching glorification of Jesus.

This explanation is basically consistent in its conception
with the argument of Vincent Taylor that although Jesus
was considered to be Messiah, at least in certain respects
by some during the time he lived, there was also a certain
retroactive meaningfulness to a number of incidents when
the facts of crucifixion and subsequent glorification made
their impact upon the consciousness of the disciples (see
e.g., John 2:19-22). This is to point out once again that
it was the things Jesus did that necessitated the further question concerning his identity.

The Temptation, 1:12, 13 (Matt. 4:1-11; Luke 4:1-13)

[12, 13] Mark's desire to get into the account of Jesus'
life and ministry caused him to be extremely brief. Where

Matthew and Luke both go into considerable detail, it may be said that Mark only mentions Jesus' temptation in passing.

There is a certain balance derived from the fact that the account of the formal temptation of Jesus is placed in the text immediately after the baptism and blessing. It should be evident that Jesus' earthly life was not designed to be self-satisfying. It is significant that, according to Mark, Satan is not said to leave Jesus after the temptation as he does in the parallel accounts (Matt. 4:11; Luke 4:13). Indeed, this first confrontation between Jesus and Satan marks the beginning of a long-term engagement. Mark enlarges on this point later (see 3:22-27). The central concern is that it was necessary for Jesus to undergo certain trials if he were to establish his authority or right (*exousia*) to serve as a sacrifice for man.

This lengthy temptation in the wilderness should be thought of as a real and genuine struggle with the forces of evil (see Heb. 2:14-18). It must never be considered as a sham struggle in which Jesus could not really have sinned because he was the Son of God. His temptation to failure must have been real in every respect. He could not have been assisted by anything which is not available to every other man in his temptation. Unless Jesus' temptation was completely real, the salvation offered to mankind is incomplete.

Mark's account of the temptation is in fact so abbreviated that if it were not for the parallel accounts one would not know how the story came out. The significant point is that it is the Spirit who **drove** Jesus into the wilderness to do battle with Satan. Mark's more complete explanation may be found later (3:17-30). Jesus cast out demons by the Holy Spirit. This could only be done after he had bound Satan (3:22f.). That was accomplished in the temptation. The exorcisms which occurred later are therefore to be understood as mopping-up operations. It was as Son of God (1:11) that Jesus went into the desert to battle Satan and he is confessed as such in the later exorcisms (1:24; 3:11; 5:7).

Mark's urgency to enter into a discussion about the deeds of Jesus' ministry is evidenced by the fact that in thirteen verses he disposes of approximately nine-tenths of

¹⁴ Now after John was arrested, Jesus came into Galilee, preaching the gospel of God, ¹⁵ and saying, "The time is fulfilled, and the kingdom of God is at hand; repent, and believe in the gospel."

Jesus' life. He then turns to an examination of the deeds of the ministry. Mark must have been strongly motivated toward his purpose in order for him to have encompassed so much in such a short space. It must be repeated that his goal was to record Jesus' activities in such a way that when the account was read, it would stir men's hearts toward belief. Simply put, it would appear that Mark wanted faith to be the result of the reading of his Gospel (cf. John 20:30f.).

THE GALILEAN MINISTRY, 1:14—8:26
The Beginning, 1:14, 15 (Matt. 4:12-17; Luke 4:14, 15)

[14, 15] The essential message of Jesus' early ministry is here summarized in terms of two announcements and two commands. Jesus first urged that **the time is fulfilled.** This must simply mean that all the necessary preparations and preliminaries had been completed and that the next event could only be the "breaking-in" of the **kingdom** (*basileia,* reign or rule) of God. This is the declaration couched in the second statement that **the kingdom of God is at hand.** In one way of speaking, Jesus' second observation is an interpretation or further expansion of the first.

In the past God had often been referred to as Israel's King, and they as his people (1 Sam. 12:12; Isa. 41:21; 43:15; Jer. 8:19). Even when Israel had its own king he ruled "in the name of God." This was, of course, a somewhat limited concept of God's relation with his people and therefore it was not uncommon for Israel's future to be ideally conceived, particularly by the prophets, as a time when God's reign would be completely acknowledged. Associated with this concept came to be an expectation of an ideal, duly anointed ruler. This "anointed one" (Hebrew, *Messiah;* Greek, *Christ*) was to make God's presence felt in a completely new way.

The observations noted by Jesus made action imperative.

25

That is, repentance and faith were necessary because the kingdom was upon them. The Greek verb translated **is at hand** perhaps should be rendered here "has come near." And although this may be understood in a temporal sense, i.e., as "imminent," it may here be used more in its spatial sense. The emphasis would then be upon the very presence of Jesus as an embodiment of the kingdom.

Repent is literally "change your mind," but in biblical usage indicates a complete redirection or restructuring of life. Belief **in the gospel** must be belief that the things due to take place would, in fact, occur. Inasmuch as Jesus had not completed his sacrifice for man, his preaching and his commands at this point must have been very much like those of John the Baptist. It should be remembered that the ministries of both John and Jesus were preparatory to the establishment of the church. The primary difference between the two lies in the fact that Jesus' ministry occurred farther along the historical line of development (see Luke 16:16 and Matt. 10:11ff.), and therefore belief in future potentialities was progressively becoming belief in (sometimes knowledge of) past occurrences. Belief itself was a principal part of the developing revelation, regardless of the point at which one might have found himself.

The Call of the First Disciples, 1:16-20 (Matt. 4:18-22; Luke 5:1-11)

One of the striking things about Jesus' ministry has always been its "veiledness." Its obscure and remote beginnings have surely contributed to this, but Jesus himself never seems to have approached his work with any great desire to impress people. His desire rather was to let his work stand for itself. He did not attempt to attract people for any other reason than to lead them to the conviction that he was the Son of God. Ultimately this concept of sonship is the only legitimate reason for following Jesus. This is extremely important, especially in attempting to give character to a formal Christology.

In the gradual unfolding of Jesus' purpose, however, it is possible to see a certain, almost deliberate, movement. If Mark's Gospel is characterized as a movement toward Jerusalem and crucifixion, then the first step was Jesus'

¹⁶ And passing along by the Sea of Galilee, he saw Simon and Andrew the brother of Simon casting a net in the sea; for they were fishermen. ¹⁷ And Jesus said to them, "Follow me and I will make you become fishers of men." ¹⁸ And immediately they left their nets and followed him. ¹⁹ And going on a little farther, he saw James the son of Zebedee and John his brother, who were in their boat mending the nets. ²⁰ And immediately he called them; and they left their father Zebedee in the boat with the hired servants, and followed him.

---

approach toward the fishermen of Galilee. These "uneducated, common men" were destined to become the very backbone of his ministry.

It is worthy of note that, according to Mark, Jesus' first disciples were called before witnessing any miracles or before there had been any opportunity to teach them about the nature of his kingdom. This is even more remarkable when it is remembered that the Gospel as a whole seems to be designed to impress the reader with regard to Jesus' identity by means of reiterating his deeds. Here these men respond simply because of the demand placed on them by the announcement or proclamation that the kingdom was upon them.

[16-19] The call of these four fishermen, Simon, Andrew, James, and John, is divided into two parts. Jesus found the first pair of brothers fishing with their nets **in the sea.** The second pair he found with their father **in their boat mending the nets.** It is interesting to note that even among these fishermen there was a certain difference in economic standing. Simon and Andrew seem to have had only the barest minimum of equipment, whereas James and John may, in fact, have come from a fairly well established family group with "hired servants" (vs. 20).

[20] Perhaps the most striking element in this story is the fact that these disciples seem **immediately** to have left their occupation to follow Jesus. The verb follow (*akolouthein,* vss. 18 and 20) should be taken here to mean "become a disciple of." It is not simply suggestive of companionship. Many have hastily concluded that these men dropped what they were doing and went with Jesus never to return to their nets again. This is surely incorrect. The

²¹ And they went into Capernaum; and immediately on the sabbath he entered the synagogue and taught. ²² And they were astonished at his teaching, for he taught them as one who had authority, and not as the scribes. ²³ And immediately there was in their synagogue a man with an unclean spirit; ²⁴ and he cried out, "What have you to do with us, Jesus of Nazareth? Have you come to destroy us? I know who you are, the Holy One of God."

---

disciples are found fishing later in the ministry of Jesus and even after his resurrection (see John 21). The more correct picture is that although they became Jesus' disciples, they did not leave their fishing in any final sense. Only as the demands of discipleship became greater would they have been found fishing less and less. The fact that their devotion to Jesus was a gradually increasing thing should not be allowed to discredit the genuineness and real depth that it did possess.

The Demoniac in the Synagogue, 1:21-28 (Luke 4:31-37)

It should be pointed out that the story of the man with the unclean spirit is the first of a series of five healing narratives, which is climaxed by the story of the paralytic in the opening verses of chapter two. The most important teaching in the wider section is to be found in the last narrative. The stories appearing between the man with the unclean spirit and the paralytic seem to serve as a means of building up the importance of the wider and certainly more important conclusions. These have to do primarily with Jesus' right or authority (1:22) to forgive sins (2:10).

The Mediterranean civilizations of Jesus' time understood the world to be filled with great numbers of disembodied spirits or demons. These were considered to be a part of the forces of evil. In Jewish thought they would probably have been roughly conceived as counterparts to the angels who served the Lord. They are characterized in several different ways in the Gospels. In addition to the proclaiming type that is found in this passage, there are also dumb (Matt. 9:32ff.) and "epileptic" spirits (Matt. 17:14ff.).

[21-24] Jesus was in the **synagogue,** probably because

28

he found the atmosphere there good for his teaching.
Although the teaching seems to have led to Jesus' encounter
with the demon, Mark apparently considered the incident
a part of the **teaching** (see vs. 27) and a demonstration of
its **authority.**

Here, reference must be made to two points considered
in the Introduction: the messianic awareness of the demons, and the role these narratives seem to play in the
structure of Mark's Gospel. The demon's statement, **I
know who you are, the Holy One of God,** contains a confession and a messianic recognition. This is true, that is,
if **Holy One** *(hagios)* equals "Anointed One" *(christos,* see
John 6:69; Acts 2:27; 3:14). Such a recognition on the
part of the demon might be credited to some sort of supernatural evil power. Such is surely one possible interpretation. Although admittedly difficult to understand, this
awareness seems to cause the demon narratives in
Mark to contribute to the revealing of Jesus' identity
as this theme appears in the "plot" of the Gospels (see
Introduction, p. 14).

In any case, this confession infers the fact that Jesus had
the power to overcome all wrong and evil. This is one of the
fundamental points. It should also be noted that these evil
powers, consistently conceived as oppressive in nature, are,
from a practical point of view, destroyed in Jesus. The **spirit**
was **unclean** in the sense that it separated the man from God,
but Jesus brought the spirit under God's rule. Gospel
stories such as this typify, in their way, Jesus' final conquer-
ing of all things. Even the questions, **What have you to do with
us?** and **Have you come to destroy us?** fit into this pattern (see
esp. 3:27). They might even be more emphatic if conceived
as statements rather than questions.

The authority of Jesus' **teaching** was impressive, so much
so that the unclean spirits could not resist his command.
This description of Jesus' **teaching** is offered to the reader
as being directly opposite to that of the scribes (vs. 22).
What is more, after the unclean spirit was cast out, the
bystanders found it necessary to describe this **teaching** as
new. This should probably be taken as a way of describing
a new plateau in their understanding of Jesus. The striking
character of Mark's description here is underlined by Luke's

²⁵ But Jesus rebuked him, saying, "Be silent, and come out of him!" ²⁶ And the unclean spirit, convulsing him and crying with a loud voice, came out of him. ²⁷ And they were all amazed, so that they questioned among themselves, saying, "What is this? A new teaching! With authority he commands even the unclean spirits, and they obey him." ²⁸ And at once his fame spread everywhere throughout all the surrounding region of Galilee.

²⁹ And immediately he′ left the synagogue, and entered the house of Simon and Andrew, with James and John. ³⁰ Now Simon's mother-in-law lay sick with a fever, and immediately they told him of her. ³¹ And he came and took her by the hand and lifted her up, and the fever left her; and she served them.

′ Other ancient authorities read *they*

---

use of "word" (*logos*, Luke 4:36) for the Markan teaching (*didachē*).

[25-28] Jesus' reaction, when one might have expected otherwise, was to rebuke the spirit, commanding silence and ordering him to come out of the man. The spirit had no alternative. Such an incident attracted the attention of people throughout the surrounding area. The fact that Jesus' reputation spread rapidly after such incidents has caused certain commentators to conclude that his command to silence was a way of encouraging the spread of his message. Surely Jesus' purpose was more carefully planned than that.

Peter's Mother-in-law, 1:29-31 (Matt. 8:14, 15; Luke 4:38, 39)

[29-31] This story concerning Simon (Peter) follows immediately the incident in the synagogue. As the incident does not add to the wider narrative in any readily apparent way, it must be associated with the Petrine origin of the Gospel (see Introduction, p. 7f.). It is without doubt told from Peter's point of view. Cranfield (p. 81) observes, "Significantly the detail concerns not the sickness and its cure, but rather unimportant matters which would nevertheless be of special interest to the people involved."

Jesus went from the synagogue to the house of Peter and Andrew. Peter's mother-in-law was sick with a fever, and it was only natural that they should tell Jesus about

³² **That evening, at sundown, they brought to him all who
were sick or possessed with demons. ³³ And the whole city
was gathered together about the door. ³⁴ And he healed many
who were sick with various diseases, and cast out many
demons; and he would not permit the demons to speak, because
they knew him.**

---

her illness. The text implies that they expected him to do
something about it. In what can only impress one as
immediate action, Jesus **took her by the hand** and **lifted her
up.** The **fever** disappeared and, as a proof of her recovery,
she served them.

The fact that some of the Lord's closest followers were
married men is impressive. One can only admire their accom-
plishments the more in view of such responsibilities. In
Peter's case, some have suggested that he may have been
a widower. This, however, becomes unlikely in light of 1
Corinthians 9:5 where Paul suggests that Peter was accus-
tomed to taking his wife with him as he went about preaching.

General Healing, 1:32-34 (Matt. 8:16, 17; Luke 4:40, 41)

[32-34] Jesus' reputation seems to be rapidly building.
In another incident which Mark records as occurring the
evening after the two preceding incidents (the Jewish sabbath
having ended at **sundown**), the Gospel reports that the **whole
city** had gathered and that the people were **about the door.**
Their response to Jesus' earlier healings is demonstrated
in the fact that they brought many who were **sick** or distressed. Jesus responded to their requests and many were
relieved of their burdens. The most striking aspect of these
demon narratives continues to be that the demons recognized
Jesus. That is to say, they **knew him** to be the Christ, as
was the case with the man in the synagogue. Once again
Jesus demanded their silence. One can only conclude, whatever Jesus' specific motivation, that he demanded their silence for the sake of achieving his greater purpose. That
is, Jesus must be viewed as commanding only that which
would ultimately lead the greatest number to understand
that he was God's Anointed and that, as such, he could
offer the final solution to their most pressing problem.

³⁵ And in the morning, a great while before day, he rose and went out to a lonely place, and there he prayed. ³⁶ And Simon and those who were with him pursued him, ³⁷ and they found him and said to him, "Everyone is searching for you." ³⁸ And he said to them, "Let us go on to the next towns, that I may preach there also; for that is why I came out." ³⁹ And he went throughout all Galilee, preaching in their synagogues and casting out demons.

Retreat, 1:35-39 (Luke 4:42-44)

[35] After the third successive miraculous incident, Jesus found it necessary to withdraw and pray. He rose a **great while** before sunrise and went out to a deserted place. The fact that he felt such a need is impressive. His humanity again manifests itself; he needed the refreshing experience. Such an incident also indicates something of his relationship with his Father. Even though the passage does not give much detail, an intimacy does pervade it. Jesus approached his Father as an obedient son in need of blessing.

As there is no open reference to stress of any sort in the passage, one is at first inclined to interpret it in terms of practical necessity. That is, that the praying Jesus should be seen much as the devout praying Christian. Mark, however, only rarely associates prayer with Jesus (see 6:46 and 14:32ff.), and considerable stress is mentioned in both the other passages as being a part of Jesus' burden. In contrast Luke is well known for mentioning prayer in a number of other places which also reflect a number of different circumstances. One is therefore drawn toward the conclusion that prayer, wherever mentioned by Mark, should be taken as an indication of serious burden and may have to do with Jesus' divine purpose.

[36-39] It was not long, however, until Jesus was missed, and Peter led the group to find him. Peter urged that **everyone** was looking for him. One wonders to what extent it was Peter himself who was in need of the Lord's presence. Jesus refused the suggestion to return. It was his desire to go elsewhere and preach. He said, **Let us go on to the next towns, that I may preach there also; for this is why I came out.** This statement is one of two (cf. 2:17) in Mark's Gospel

⁴⁰ And a leper came to him beseeching him, and kneeling said to him, "If you will, you can make me clean." ⁴¹ Moved with pity, he stretched out his hand and touched him, and said to him, "I will; be clean." ⁴² And immediately the leprosy left him, and he was made clean. ⁴³ And he sternly charged him, and sent him away at once, ⁴⁴ and said to him, "See that you say nothing to any one; but go, show yourself to the priest, and offer for your cleansing what Moses commanded, for a proof to the people."ᶠ ⁴⁵ But he went out and began to talk freely about it, and to spread the news, so that Jesusᵍ could no longer openly enter a town, but was out in the country; and people came to him from every quarter.

ᶠ Greek *to them*

ᵍ Greek *he*

---

in which Jesus, in the first person, directly states his purpose on earth. In a context primarily given over to healing narratives, it can only be of extreme significance that Jesus says that he should be preaching. This is surely an indication of his own conception of his basic work, and is consistent with the view of Jesus as teacher elsewhere in the context.

The Curing of a Leper, 1:40-45 (Matt. 8:1-4; Luke 5:12-16)

[40-42] The fourth healing narrative in the sequence concerns a leper. Jesus' reputation as a healer is evident in the fact that the leper came to Jesus himself and said, **If you will, you can make me clean.** The leper's action must in some sense be considered an act of faith. The passage does not, however, mention the fact. The text does reveal that Jesus was moved with compassion and because of that healed the man. In this connection it should be noted that Mark shows special interest in Jesus' touching sufferers (7:33; 8:22) or their touching him (3:10; 5:27f., 30f.; 6:56). The passage further indicates, by a typically emphatic Markan term, that this was done **immediately.**

[43-45] Jesus sent the man to the **priest** for the ritual inspection and sacrifice (Lev. 14:2ff.). Although Jesus was not uncritical of the law, especially as an end in itself (see Mark 2:27f., Matt. 5:17ff.), he seems to have been raised in the main to keep the ritual law. The evidence in the Gospels for this point is clear (Luke 2:21ff., 41; Matt. 17:24ff.; see also Mark 7:1-23; 10:1-12, 19-21), although Jesus

is more often remembered for his castigation of superficiality as it appeared in the scribes and Pharisees.

In a manner similar to that found in the earlier demon incident (vs. 34), Jesus strictly charges silence (see Introduction, p. 13f.). The man was told in the most direct terms that he was not to speak to anyone. He disregarded the command and freely talked about the incident. The news spread rapidly and the result mentioned in the text was that Jesus could no longer go about easily. It is at this point that Jesus' ministry seems most like that of John the Baptist, for the text says that the people went out in the country to Jesus.

The significance of this story should not be underestimated. Jesus touched the leper (vs. 41), which was in itself extremely provocative to the Jews. The healing of lepers belonged to the eschaton or end-time (Matt. 11:5; Luke 7:22). The disciples' healing was thought of similarly (Matt. 10:8). Jesus was disturbed because, in Jewish thought, diseases were the work of Satan; therefore Jesus' anger is like that directed at the demons (1:25; 3:12; 9:25). The **people** (*autois*, vs. 44) were those concerned with the law, that is, the religious establishment. **Proof** has the meaning "witness for the prosecution." In the very performance of the miracle Jesus showed his attitude toward the law, abiding by and challenging it at the same time.

In all of this, the pericope represents an advance over verses 21-28. There Jesus healed on the sabbath, but Mark showed no interest in the legal problems involved (cf. 3:2ff.). Apparently he wanted to establish Jesus' authority first; then followed the manifestation (vs. 44). These two incidents lay the foundation for the conflict stories which follow (2:1—3:6).

The Paralytic, 2:1-12 (Matt. 9:1-8; Luke 5:17-26)

The story of the paralytic in these opening verses of chapter two plays a dual role. It is the last of five healing narratives which began with the story of the demoniac (1:21-28). It is at the same time the first in a series of five "conflict" stories (2:1—3:6), three of which involve miracles, that lead up to the first suggestion in the Gospel that Jesus should be destroyed. The dominant theme in the first series is not

¹ And when he returned to Capernaum after some days, it was reported that he was at home. ² And many were gathered together, so that there was no longer room for them, not even about the door; and he was preaching the word to them. ³ And they came, bringing to him a paralytic carried by four men. ⁴ And when they could not get near him because of the crowd, they removed the roof above him; and when they had made an opening, they let down the pallet on which the paralytic lay.

---

so much Jesus' "power" and exercise of authority over human physical problems as it is his ultimate authority over sin. This may be graphically seen in the paragraph at hand. The "conflict" that appears in the second series is the result of the earlier manifestation of Jesus' power. That is, the things that Jesus did and taught began to irritate, and eventually points of conflict arose. These then were the specific points at issue between Jesus and the religious leaders of the Jews. The story of the paralytic is one of the most open and straightforward declarations of both Jesus' power and purpose (albeit, in conflict) that may be found in the Gospel, and there can be no reasonable doubt that Mark prepared the way for this last story with the other stories of similar nature which precede it.

[1-4] Consider the situation: it had been reported that Jesus was **at home** in Capernaum. On hearing this report the four men who carried the paralytic, as well as the paralytic himself, were moved to action. The obvious organization in their movement would seem to imply that they had been waiting for such an opportunity, but, it should be considered as the action of five men and not four. It is unlikely that the four men would have moved without the consent of the paralytic himself. It would be easier to think that the paralytic was the leader of the group. The reference to **their faith** (vs. 5) embraces the complete group.

The men found Jesus completely surrounded and therefore found it impossible to bring their sick friend to him immediately. One can only imagine in such a situation that the crowd gathered must have been either of tremendous size or of a very unusual character, for the tendency in most crowds is to make way easily for the sick. Since this

⁵ And when Jesus saw their faith, he said to the paralytic, "My son, your sins are forgiven." ⁶ Now some of the scribes were sitting there, questioning in their hearts, ⁷ "Why does this man speak thus? It is blasphemy! Who can forgive sins but God alone?" ⁸ And immediately Jesus, perceiving in his spirit that they thus questioned within themselves, said to them, "Why do you question thus in your hearts? ⁹ Which is easier, to say to the paralytic, 'Your sins are forgiven,' or to say, 'Rise, take up your pallet and walk'? ¹⁰ But that you may know that the Son of man has authority on earth to forgive sins"—he said to the paralytic—

---

did not occur here, some special set of circumstances must be implied.

The four men were not easily put off. They fell on the idea of **removing** (literally, "digging out") **the roof** and lowering their friend down to Jesus. Such would not have been an extremely difficult task in view of the semi-permanent roofs made of sticks and hardened earth that were common in the area at the time. Nevertheless, it must have been quite an impressive sight for the crowd to see the roof torn away and a man lowered through the opening. The boldness of their act indicates the depth of their concern and their commitment to a plan of action.

[5-10] There were both friends and enemies of Jesus in the crowd, and the situation gave him the opportunity of confirming the one and, at least to some degree, clarifying the opposition of the other. He was, in the process of revealing himself, intruding more and more into their awareness. Ultimately, of course, he intended to force a decision about himself, his person, and his mission. His first step in achieving this was to say to the paralytic, **My son, your sins are forgiven.** It should be urged in the strongest possible terms that the healing did not occur at this point. Two separate and distinct things happened to this man; they should not in any way be blurred into one.

The reaction of the scribes, of course, was to question Jesus' right to declare forgiveness. They objected that **God alone** could **forgive sins.** They were right. That is, they asked the right question, but out of the wrong motivation. If they had only questioned further, "Could this be God?" how

[11] "I say to you, rise, take up your pallet and go home."
[12] And he rose, and immediately took up the pallet and went out before them all; so that they were all amazed and glorified God, saying, "We never saw anything like this!"

---

drastically different the whole course of the story might have been.

Jesus had created the desired reaction, and at this point his questions and the **Son of man** sayings enter the picture (vs. 10). The occurrences of the Son of man sayings in the Gospel are discussed in the comments on 2:28. The declaration associated with **Son of man** has to do with the fact that he (Son of man—Jesus) does have **authority** (*exousia*) to forgive sins. Jesus brought the power of forgiveness to men who were in the power of sin. This is the message of the Gospel story. It was a messianic function to bring forgiveness of sins. That forgiveness comes through Jesus was a key issue separating the church from Judaism. He asked whether it was **easier** to say to the paralytic that he should rise, or to say to him that his sins were forgiven. The point is that it was just as easy to say the one as the other, meaning that it was just as easy for the Son of man to forgive sins as it was for him to heal. But to prove that he had the right or **authority** to forgive sins, he healed the paralytic.

[11, 12] It must be said emphatically again that this is the second thing done for the paralytic. First his sins were forgiven, then Jesus healed him. Jesus himself says that he did the latter to prove he had the right to do the former. Although it could not be proved in many cases because of the nature of the evidence, it is tempting to argue that all of Jesus' miracles had the primary purpose of demonstrating his right or power in other areas, indeed, his divine purpose. It is at least correct to urge that his healing work was never central to his ministry. The earlier miracles had said something about who Jesus was. This one says something about what he does for man. But the deed is not merely humanitarian: forgiveness has eschatological implications.

The exit of the paralytic, walking and carrying his pallet, must have been a thunderous conclusion in the eyes of the

¹³ **He went out again beside the sea; and all the crowd gathered about him, and he taught them.** ¹⁴ **And as he passed on, he saw Levi the son of Alphaeus sitting at the tax office, and he said to him, "Follow me." And he rose and followed him.**

---

crowd. Overwhelmed with amazement, they declared, **We never saw anything like this!**

The Call of Levi, 2:13-17 (Matt. 9:9-13; Luke 5:27-32)

[13, 14] Here **Levi** is called **the son of Alphaeus.** In the Matthean parallel the name mentioned is Matthew, not **Levi.** This has regularly been resolved as two names for the same person, a phenomenon not uncommon in the Bible. This particular incident is complicated, however, by the fact that Matthew is mentioned later in Mark (3:18), but that same reference also speaks of James as **the son of Alphaeus.** Whether Levi and James were brothers or whether Levi equals Matthew must, it appears, remain a slight uncertainty.

Jesus is now well into his ministry. It will not be uncommon in the months to come to find large crowds gathered about him, and, as will be seen a number of times, it will be customary to find him teaching. Jesus **passed on** from the teaching situation, saw Levi at his tax-collector's post, and commanded him to **follow.** The text seems to indicate that he **followed** immediately. This is borne out by the fact that Jesus is seen in the following verses eating a meal with Levi and his friends at Levi's house.

It is not uncommon to find this passage interpreted in such a way that it is made to suggest that Jesus had the power in his own person to overwhelm a man; that, when he commanded, a man had no choice but to follow. This must be wrong. Although such a device may have been used to elicit attention, it would not be seemly for Jesus to require individuals to follow him on the strength of an overwhelming personality. The only legitimate reason one may have for following him is that he believes that he is the Son of God. The only genuinely Christian view of Christ is one that sets him up as Lord and Savior because of the

38

¹⁵ And as he sat at table in his house, many tax collectors and sinners were sitting with Jesus and his disciples; for there were many who followed him. ¹⁶ And the scribes ^h of the Pharisees, when they saw that he was eating with sinners and tax collectors, said to his disciples, "Why does he eat ⁱ with tax collectors and sinners?" ¹⁷ And when Jesus heard it, he said to them, "Those who are well have no need of a physician, but those who are sick; I came not to call the righteous, but sinners."

^h Other ancient authorities read *and*
ⁱ Other ancient authorities add *and drink*

conviction that he was and is the Son of God. If it is held that Jesus would not have exercised his personality in this way, one can only conclude that Matthew had known at least something about Jesus earlier (see e.g., vs. 13). The intimacy in the following verses might suggest a relationship that had had some period of time to develop.

[15-17] Verse fifteen particularly describes what seems to be a casual social situation. It is certainly not strained with formality. The statement is literally "he reclined," the usual posture for taking a meal. The suggestion in the end that **many followed him** indicates that it was not a planned gathering and may therefore be more properly viewed as a sort of spontaneous gathering of friends.

It is only natural to expect the **scribes** who were Pharisees, as most were, to object to this kind of table fellowship (see Vol. 1 for background on the Pharisees). The Pharisees in particular were careful about the ceremonial defilement which came from association with those who did not keep the ritual law as carefully as they. This, of course, cut directly against Jesus' understanding of his own life and purpose. One of the recurring complaints against him was his contact with **sinners,** i.e., those who were not in strict conformity with the law. It is in this set of circumstances that Jesus makes his second and final first person declaration of his purpose (cf. 1:38). He began by making the obvious observation that physicians devote their attention to the sick and not to those who are well. He drives his analogy home by saying, **I came not to call the righteous**

¹⁸ Now John's disciples and the Pharisees were fasting; and people came and said to him, "Why do John's disciples and the disciples of the Pharisees fast, but your disciples do not fast?" ¹⁹ And Jesus said to them, "Can the wedding guests fast while the bridegroom is with them? As long as they have the bridegroom with them, they cannot fast. ²⁰ The days will come, when the bridegroom is taken away from them, and then they will fast in that day.

---

but sinners. It should be obvious that to **call . . . sinners** is another way of saying that he came to preach (1:38).

The Question of Fasting, 2:18-22 (Matt. 9:14-17; Luke 5:33-39)

[18] The discussion continues of various themes involving conflict. The people around Jesus reflect that it was a religious custom for Jews to **fast.** At the time some of them fasted twice a week (Luke 18:12). Here attention is called to the fact that both the **disciples of the Pharisees** and those **of John** made a regular habit of this form of self-deprivation. They wonder why Jesus' **disciples** do not follow the same practice and therefore they raised this question. Fasting was just one of the items of religious practice which distinguished the life style of Jesus and his disciples. Differences in this regard continued to separate Christians and Jews.

[19, 20] Jesus observes simply that it was not in order. That is to say, it would be as illogical for his disciples to fast, as it would be for a guest or friend to fast at a wedding celebration. For one thing, fasting was a sign of mourning. Jesus as the **bridegroom** brings the joy of the Messianic Age by his presence. His analogy is even more impressive when one remembers that it was customary at the time for a wedding celebration to last several days. There would have been ample time therefore in the course of the average "feast" to arrange at least a brief "fast." It is obvious, however, that a fast would be out of place anywhere in the course of normal wedding festivities. So also, it is out of order for Jesus' disciples as long as he is with them.

Jesus indicates that the time will come when the bride-

²¹ **No one sews a piece of unshrunk cloth on an old garment; if he does, the patch tears away from it, the new from the old, and a worse tear is made. ²² And no one puts new wine into old wineskins; if he does, the wine will burst the skins, and the wine is lost, and so are the skins; but new wine is for fresh skins.''** ʲ

ʲ Other ancient authorities omit *but new wine is for fresh skins*

---

groom will indeed be **taken away from them,** and fasting will take place then. Many commentators have seen here Jesus' first prophetic indication of his own suffering, even though the passage is admittedly ambiguous in this regard. That is, it is uncertain that Jesus is saying that *he* will be **taken away** (see Isa. 53:8). One cannot be sure, but it does seem that Jesus is putting into the minds of his followers the possibility that he will be **taken.** This may be viewed as some sort of preparation for the more severe things that were to happen to him later. One must be careful not to interpret an incident in terms of what he knows happened at a later date. The passage must be examined primarily in terms of the situation in which the incident originally occurred.

[**21, 22**] Jesus closes the incident by suggesting that one would not put an **unshrunk** patch on an **old garment** for fear of damaging the garment even more; likewise, one would not put **new wine** into **old** skins fearing similar consequences. An old garment with a hole in it has become weak. An unshrunk patch in the process of shrinking would only tend to tear the garment further. Wine was put into new skins mainly because in the process of fermentation there was a slight increase in the bulk of the wine which stretched the skin. An old skin would not tolerate a second stretching. Therefore, new wine was put into new skins.

The simple purpose of these two figures is to emphasize the newness of the kingdom of God. In a sense the "breaking in" of the kingdom of God was a fulfillment of the law (Matt. 5:17). While true, this is mainly a way of thinking, for the law in may ways had been or was in the process of being put away. In suggesting that there comes a time

²³ **One sabbath he was going through the grainfields; and as they made their way his disciples began to pluck heads of grain. ²⁴ And the Pharisees said to him, "Look, why are they doing what is not lawful on the sabbath?"**

---

when a man must purchase a new garment and acquire a new wineskin, Jesus is saying that what he is announcing—the kingdom of God—is new and the old must give place to it.

The Lord of the Sabbath, 2:23-28 (Matt. 12:1-8; Luke 6:1-5)

Laws concerning the sabbath (Ex. 23:12; Deut. 5:14) were the source of uneasy relationships between Jesus and certain Jewish groups a number of times in the course of his ministry. The last two incidents in the present series of conflict stories involve some of these "laws." Later rejection of sabbath-keeping by the Gentile/Christian church made preservation of stories reflecting Jesus' attitude toward the sabbath important.

[23, 24] In the first story of sabbath conflict, Jesus' disciples show a normal bodily need in that they were hungry. The fact that they were driven to gather some unharvested grain for themselves may indicate that the circumstances were at least difficult, if not extreme. Jewish law permitted one passing through another's property to pick what he could gather in his hand (Deut. 23:24f.). In this particular incident Jesus was not deliberate in his attempt to provoke discussion about the sabbath. Nevertheless, the confrontation between Jesus and his critics is quite real.

The law forbade work on the sabbath. The points of issue here, however, do not contain direct reference to the commands to observe the sabbath but rather were concerned with various traditions associated with sabbath observance. What the disciples did was interpreted as reaping (Ex. 34:21). The fact that the Pharisees would raise a question about the action of Jesus' disciples reflects an extreme and technical interpretation of the law. The Pharisees were noted, of course, for their attitudes in this regard. Several hundred laws regarding various types of situations had evolved in their tradition through the cen-

[25] And he said to them, "Have you never read what David did, when he was in need and was hungry, he and those who were with him: [26] how he entered the house of God, when Abiathar was high priest, and ate the bread of the Presence, which it is not lawful for any but the priests to eat, and also gave it to those who were with him?" [27] And he said to them, "The sabbath was made for man, not man for the sabbath; [28] so the Son of man is lord even of the sabbath."

---

turies. Their attitude at this point was very legalistic in its attempt to perform all the normal functions of the day—all of which were considered to be a part of their religious life—perfectly and in accordance with the "law."

[25, 27] In justifying the situation, Jesus suggests that David once ate the bread which was intended for the high priest. It may be significant that Jesus cites an incident involving such an Old Testament great; that is, there were others that he could have used. In any case, there appears to be a slip here with regard to detail. **Abiathar** was high priest during David's reign (2 Sam. 15:35); but it was his father, Ahimelech, who was priest in the time that David ate the consecrated bread (1 Sam. 21:1-6). Although Abiathar was not actually the high priest when David ate the **bread of the presence,** it was in the same time period (translating, "in the time of Abiathar the high priest"). Perhaps the problem should be solved in some such way. This sort of thing should not, however, be allowed to cloud the clarity of the point being made. Human need takes precedence over ritual law. Moreover, the sabbath was designed for the good of man, not to be a burden on him (see below).

[28] The **Son of man** saying at the end of the paragraph, the second in the Gospel, may be taken in two ways. That is, it may or may not involve some kind of messianic declaration. Either alternative is possible on the basis of the text and what is known about the original Aramaic expression.

No New Testament subject has received more attention in recent years than the Son of man sayings. The problem is so complex that any detailed discussion of it must be omitted here. **Son of man** here may simply mean "man" (see Ps. 8; Dan. 7; Ezek. *passim*). There is no doubt that this was one of the uses of the phrase. If the expression is taken in this way, Jesus is saying that man himself is greater than any religious institution and that religious laws were made for the benefit of his own self-expression, not to enslave him in any legalistic type of ritual. This interpretation contains an obvious truth and relates the declaration to the preceding statements.

It may be, however, that something more is being said. Jesus may have selected David's example because both he and Jesus stood in the messianic lineage, Jesus himself being the end point. If the expression **Son of man** is taken in a messianic sense (see Dan. 7), then Jesus seems to be saying that he, as Messiah, has a right to call ritualistic sabbath laws into question (again see Matt. 5:17). The incident then would involve an expression on Jesus' part of his desire to reconstruct Jewish forms of worship. This, of course, would fit with the sayings concerning patching a garment and making wine found earlier in the chapter. It would also demonstrate the pointedness of Jesus' teaching in a far wider context than would the first interpretation. And, it would be in accordance with usage found later in the Gospels (see 8:31).

A word must be added concerning the sequence and placing of the **Son of man** sayings in Mark's Gospel. Of fourteen, only two occur before Peter's confession (8:27ff.), and both of these are found in chapter two, the first in connnection with the paralytic (vs. 10), the second in the paragraph under consideration. The expression is used in Mark primarily to contain and develop the concepts of suffering (see notes on 8:31ff.) and exaltation.

If the story of the paralytic is out of chronological sequence (see Introduction), as it may be, and the sabbath saying applies only to man, then it may be that there are no genuine occurrences of the phrase "Son of man" as a title prior to Peter's confession. If these things are true, the association with suffering and exaltation is all the more emphatic. It is, of course, obvious that there was no point for Jesus to suggest that he was to suffer until his followers understood

¹ Again he entered the synagogue, and a man was there
who had a withered hand. ² And they watched him, to see
whether he would heal him on the sabbath, so that they might
accuse him. ³ And he said to the man who had the withered
hand, "Come here." ⁴ and he said to them, "Is it lawful on
the sabbath to do good or to do harm, to save life or to
kill?" But they were silent.

---

who he was. That is, many men died on Roman crosses;
this one is of the most extreme importance not simply
because of his death but because of who it was that died.
Once again, the reader is thrown back on the broadly significant question of Jesus' identity: "Who then is this?"

The Man with the Withered Hand, 3:1-6 (Matt. 12:9-14; Luke 6:6-11)

The theme of conflict reaches its climax here in the fifth
and final story of the series. The sabbath is again in question.

[1-4] It would appear that Jesus' critics had come to
the synagogue for no other purpose than to watch him to
see what he might do that they might accuse him. Although
there is nothing in the text that necessarily indicates that
Jesus exercised any miraculous power to know what these
men were thinking, such is surely implied. Jesus called the
man with the withered hand to the front of the group; then
he addressed a question, not to the man, but to his own
critics, **Is it lawful on the sabbath to do good or to do harm,
to save life or to kill?** The Pharisees felt that anything that
was not urgent in "saving life" (on the sabbath) fell under
the prohibition of "work." In this case, their view would
have been that a few hours would not make that much difference. Lawful observance of the sabbath would also
praise God. The question asked here by Jesus could only
cause silence. The Pharisees could not associate themselves
with either answer. If they agreed that it was right to do
good, then they would have no grounds to criticize Jesus,
because that is what he intended to do. If they refused to
do good, which is in effect to do evil or harm, they would
certainly not appear to be just themselves. Or, on the second
horn of the dilemma, Jesus may be arraigning them on the

⁵ And he looked around at them with anger, grieved at their hardness of heart, and said to the man, "Stretch out your hand." He stretched it out, and his hand was restored. ⁶ The Pharisees went out, and immediately held counsel with the Herodians against him, how to destroy him.

---

charge of plotting against him. Jesus was willing to **save life** to the praise of God, even on the sabbath. The Pharisees were then left under the pressure of possible negative judgment not only because they were not willing to do good under these circumstances but, what is more, because they were willing to plot against an innocent man, and that on the sabbath (vss. 2, 6).

[5] Jesus looked at them **with anger, grieved at their hardness of heart.** It is, of course, quite unusual to find such language associated with Jesus. He is not often thought of as being capable of **anger.** It is interesting to note in the parallels that neither Matthew nor Luke suggest this particular emotion. There seems to have been a tendency in the later Gospel writers to soften what may have appeared to them harsh language about Jesus, language that might be misunderstood and for that reason not present a true picture.

Jesus must be thought of as having been completely both human and divine. That is, he was characterized by normal human emotions, the difference being that he always found it possible to control them. Even in this passage his anger is not in the slightest out of control (see Eph. 4:26). The thought rather seems to be that the religious superficiality of his critics tore at his very heart. They were unwilling to go beyond the legal niceties concerning the sabbath and let their religion become really meaningful to their innermost being. Under these circumstances, Jesus had no choice but to do the good deed. The man's hand **was restored.**

[6] The Pharisees, unwilling to be impressed, went away to counsel his destruction. The entrance of the concept of destruction, although one perhaps should not think in final terms just yet, completes the necessary elements of Mark's approach to the story of Jesus. At this point it is possible to see two fundamental elements: (1) Jesus' right to forgive sins

**⁷ Jesus withdrew with his disciples to the sea, and a great
multitude from Galilee followed; also from Judea ⁸ and
Jerusalem and Idumea and from beyond the Jordan and from
about Tyre and Sidon a great multitude, hearing all that he
did, came to him. ⁹ And he told his disciples to have a boat ready
for him because of the crowd, lest they should crush him;**

---

because he was the Son of God(2:10)—along with the numer-
ous elements which support this right—and (2) the ''inevitability'' of his destruction because he exercised this right.

Crowds by the Lake, 3:7-12 (Matt. 12:15-21; Luke 6:17-19)

[7, 8] In spite of the increasing conflict, indeed perhaps
to a certain extent because of it, Jesus' following continued
to grow. However, there was a difficulty. Jesus' opposition
came from more or less official sources, while his popularity
generally ran high among the common people. Eventually,
however, even this acceptance was destined to wane. Among
other things the ''official frown'' was to have its effect.
The number and distribution of the places indicated in the
text from which the people had come to Jesus shows the
extent and breadth of his following. Even at this period
he had attracted a significant amount of attention. The
clause **hearing all that he did** reveals how he gained this
popularity. Nothing is more effective than word of mouth
to convey the significance of any fact. Mark's vividness
is evident in that one can almost hear the urgency in the
voices of those whose lives had been touched by this healer.

The text says that Jesus **withdrew**. The overtone seems
to be that there were (would be) problems, if not dangers.
Matthew (12:15) goes so far as to suggest that the reason
for Jesus' withdrawal was his awareness of the destruction
plotted against him. It was, of course, of extreme importance
that Jesus be in complete control of the situation. Things
simply could not be permitted to get out of hand and cause
any of these divine events to occur prematurely.

[9] It is impressive that the people who desired to be
healed **pressed upon him to touch him.** In a similar passage,
Matthew (14:36; cf. Mark 6:56) indicates clearly that touch
was one of the means of making Jesus' power effective.
This procedure seems to be confirmed by the story of the

¹⁰ **for he had healed many, so that all who had diseases pressed upon him to touch him.** ¹¹ **And whenever the unclean spirits beheld him, they fell down before him and cried out, "You are the Son of God."** ¹² **And he strictly ordered them not to make him known.**

¹³ **And he went up on the mountain, and called to him those whom he desired; and they came to him.**

---

woman who was troubled by some type of female complication (Mark 5:24-34).

[10-12] It should be called to attention that the **unclean spirits** continue in their consistent recognition of Jesus' sonship. This is the first time however (cf. 1:24, 34) that the spirits are recorded to have specifically declared Jesus to be **the Son of God.** Earlier, it was "holy one of God." Again, any attempt fully to understand this phenomenon is met with difficulty (see Introduction, p. 13). Jesus once again demanded their silence in this matter as it would not do for them to make their understanding known. His divinity required extremely careful revelation. Such must have been very difficult to achieve.

One technical grammatical note must be mentioned at this point. It is possible that the force of "whenever" plus the verb is to suggest that everytime the spirits saw Jesus they began to speak in the way here recorded. If this interpretive insight is true, Jesus' healing ministry was much more demanding and strenuous than most have considered it.

The Choice of the Twelve, 3:13-19 (Matt. 10:2-4; Luke 6:12-16; cf. Acts 1:13)

In an ideological movement there must inevitably come the recognition and selection of intimate followers. The movement which was destined to climax in the establishment of the New Testament church was certainly no exception. The number twelve is itself obviously associated with the same number in earlier biblical contexts, particularly those involving the twelve tribes of Israel. In this way the "New Israel" began to emerge. The twelve were destined to serve as the "hard core" of God's new nation; a nation different in character but much the same in purpose.

[13] Mark records that Jesus went **up on the mountain** to

¹⁴ And he appointed twelve,ᵏ to be with him, and to be sent out to preach ¹⁵ and have authority to cast out demons: ¹⁶ Simon ᶜ whom he surnamed Peter; ¹⁷ James the son of Zebedee and John the brother of James, whom he surnamed Boanerges, that is, sons of thunder; ¹⁸ Andrew, and Philip, and Bartholomew, and Matthew, and Thomas, and James the son of Alphaeus, and Thaddaeus, and Simon the Canaanean, ¹⁹ and Judas Iscariot, who betrayed him.

ᵏ Other ancient authorities add *whom also he named apostles*
ᶜ Other authorities read *demons. ¹⁶So he appointed the twelve: Simon*

---

make his selection. With this account one is impressed that Jesus found it desirable to withdraw, presumably to put himself in the best frame of mind. It is apparent that Jesus did this sort of thing a number of times. With typical emphasis Luke (6:12) mentions that Jesus engaged in prayer prior to making his selection.

[14, 15] The passage mentions a threefold purpose in the call that Jesus issued to his followers. They were **to be with him** (form a community), **to be sent out to preach,** and **to cast out demons.** The first two of these are concerned with practicing that for which they had been prepared. The last, of course, has to do with establishing the authority of his disciples to function as his emissaries. Jesus conceived his own purpose to be bound up with preaching (see 1:38; 2:17), and for obvious reasons it was necessary to commit this responsibility to his closest followers.

Jesus' encounter with the demons has already become an important part of the story (see 1:24, 34; 3:11). These incidents, by means of encounter, put the fact of the incarnation in sharp relief. In any case, it is clear that Jesus' followers were commissioned with exactly the same duties as Jesus himself, and they were therefore faced with the same task of preaching and the same conflict with the spirits.

[16-19] The various lists of the names of the twelve do not exactly agree, as the parallel listing below makes evident.

MARK	MATTHEW	LUKE	ACTS
Peter	Peter	Peter	Peter
James	Andrew	Andrew	John
John	James	James	James
Andrew	John	John	Andrew

MARK	MATTHEW	LUKE	ACTS
Philip	Philip	Philip	Philip
Bartholomew	Bartholomew	Bartholomew	Thomas
Matthew	Thomas	Matthew	Bartholomew
Thomas	Matthew	Thomas	Matthew
James the son of Alphaeus	James the son of Alphaeus	James the son of Alphaeus	James the son of Alphaeus
Thaddaeus	Thaddaeus	Simon the Zealot	Simon the Zealot
Simon the Canaanean	Simon the Canaanean	Judas of James	Judas of James
Judas Iscariot	Judas Iscariot	Judas Iscariot	

It is possible to square certain names in the list by using one's imagination. There are, of course, varying degrees of certainty in this kind of an approach. Many commentators, however, attempt to reconcile the biblical texts in this way. One wonders if it might not be more accurate to imagine that there were some who, after being with Jesus for a time, found it imposssible to continue and it therefore became necessary to find replacements for them. There is certainly no indication anywhere in scripture that the earliest selections were necessarily final and that there could not be any later changes. At any rate, the number twelve (as noted above, to be associated with the twelve tribes of Israel, Matt. 19:28) appears to have been more important than the specific identity of those included in the group at any given time (4:10; 6:7; 9:35; 10:32; 11:11; 14:10, 17, 20, 43). In all of this, Jesus is making preparation and setting the stage for the future. In retrospect, it is now possible to see what he was doing. It was necessary, however, for the twelve themselves at that point in their development to follow in faith.

The Beelzebul Controversy, 3:20-30 (Matt. 12:22-32; Luke 11:14-23)

It has already been suggested that the most probable reaction to any hint of divine sonship from Jesus concerning self might well have been a bewildered incredulity (see Introduction). In fact, if any man were to suggest of himself that he was the "Son of God," most would respond with at least a negative shake of the head. Others would in all likelihood be even more severe. A significant number may

Then he went home; [20] and the crowd came together again, so that they could not even eat. [21] And when his family heard it, they went out to seize him, for people were saying, "He is beside himself." [22] And the scribes who came down from Jerusalem said, "He is possessed by Beelzebul, and by the prince of demons he casts out the demons." [23] And he called them to him, and said to them in parables, "How can Satan cast out Satan? [24] If a kingdom is divided against itself, that kingdom cannot stand. [25] And if a house is divided against itself, that house will not be able to stand. [26] And if Satan has risen up against himself and is divided, he cannot stand, but is coming to an end.

---

have thought Jesus to have been "out of his mind." A specific incident of such a reaction seems to appear in the text at hand. These two paragraphs are particularly important, for in them one finds alternative explanations for the conduct of Jesus—that he is not in his right mind, that he is possessed by an evil spirit, or that he is in league with Satan.

[20, 21] The phrase **he is beside himself** represents a fairly literal translation of the original. Indeed, the English idiom preserves the Greek one, "is not himself." **His family** thought to do him a service and **went out to seize him.** The verb here seems to suggest rather firm action which may indicate that they had considered the possibility of his resisting their assistance. That is, although their motives were pure, they did not know how they might be received. Attention should be called to the reference to Jesus' family. The phrase may be literally translated "those with him." It is in itself ambiguous and has been taken to refer to friends but was sometimes used of one's relatives.

[22] This interchange led to the so-called "Beelzebul controversy," the charge being that he cast out demons in the name of the prince of demons. Beelzebul does seem to be the intended name. Beelzebul or Baalzebul, "Filth-god," was apparently an intentional caricature of Baalzebub (2 Kings 1:2) which means "Fly-god."

[23-26] Jesus replied to the charge with a question, **How can Satan cast out Satan?** His argument was that if their charge were true, he was actually fighting himself and that

51

²⁷ **But no one can enter a strong man's house and plunder his goods, unless he first binds the strong man; then indeed he may plunder his house.**

²⁸ **"Truly, I say to you, all sins will be forgiven the sons of men, and whatever blasphemies they utter; ²⁹ but whoever blasphemes against the Holy Spirit never has forgiveness, but is guilty of an eternal sin"** — ³⁰ **for they had said, "He has an unclean spirit."**

---

a **kingdom** which fights against itself will fall. Likewise, **a house divided against itself** will also fall. And if Satan is fighting himself, he too will come to an end. The point is obvious: Satan is no fool. Strength lies in unity, and Satan would certainly not be the cause of civil war within his own kingdom.

[27] Jesus further makes his point by suggesting that no one would **enter a strong man's house** to **plunder** it, unless he first made sure that the strong man would not interfere. It would appear that the stronger man in the figure is Jesus himself. Indeed Jesus was in the process of taking possession of Satan's substance, a reference to his exorcisms.

[28-30] Jesus closes the incident with the problematic saying concerning the fact that men may be forgiven of everything except the sin against the Holy Spirit. Indeed, in this passage such a sin is referred to as an **eternal sin.** The word **eternal** in this context has been the source of great difficulty for many people. There have been many conscientious individuals who have intimidated themselves with the idea that they might have committed a sin for which there is no **forgiveness.** This is unfortunate, for the context makes it very clear that the so-called "unforgivable sin" is to credit the sources of evil with works which obviously belong to God. Here the scribes are confronted with mercy and love in the life of Jesus. And, although they knew that was good, they gave Satan the credit. Jesus surely has in mind an attitude of heart rather than a specific wrong deed. It is not difficult to imagine a condition of soul so corrupt that **forgiveness** is impossible, not because God is unwilling but because **forgiveness** is not desired. Christ offers no remedy for such a condition. Those who are committed

³¹ And his mother and his brothers came; and standing outside they sent to him and called him. ³² And a crowd was sitting about him;¹ and they said to him, "Your mother and your brothers are outside, asking for you." ³³ And he replied, "Who are my mother and my brothers?" ³⁴ And looking around on those who sat about him, he said, "Here are my mother and my brothers! ³⁵ Whoever does the will of God is my brother, and sister, and mother."

¹ Other early authorities add *and your sisters*

---

to a life of sin thereby fix the limits of God's grace with regard to themselves. They place themselves outside the reach of his loving concern.

It should be obvious that those who have concerned themselves most with the possiblity of having committed an eternal sin are the very ones who should, in fact, be least concerned. Needless to say, however, Satan has his way of using all otherwise good things for his purposes. That all these diverse elements belong to the same context is confirmed by verse thirty which says that Jesus responded in this way because he was charged with the possession of an unclean spirit.

That this pericope is important in understanding the way in which Jesus confronted and ultimately became victorious over the Satanic forces present in the world goes without question. Further, the incident is therefore significant in connection with Mark's literary purpose. For a discussion of these points see comments on 1:40-45.

Christ's True Kinfolk, 3:31-35 (Matt. 12:46-50; Luke 8:19-21)

[31] One has the impression that the appearance of Jesus' mother and his brothers is somehow a part of the wider context (see vs. 21). In any case, the nature of the action here may indicate that they were at least considering the possibility that the charge with regard to his sanity might be valid. To say the least, one is inclined to feel a certain sympathy coming through in their movement toward him.

[32-35] When Jesus' family (**brothers** is here taken in the literal sense; see discussion of 6:1-6) found him, there was a crowd about him, and they were unable to approach

him directly. Jesus was told that they were outside. When he heard it he took the opportunity to teach a lesson. Somewhat startling in its approach, but surely extremely effective, Jesus suggested that his true family consisted of those who **do the will of God.**

One is reluctant to imagine Jesus in this way actually rejecting his earthly family. Although there is certainly no evidence in the paragraph, one feels confident that Jesus would not have severed family ties unnecessarily. The fact that his family appears later in the gospel story would seem to confirm this conclusion. Such a feeling should not, however, be allowed to undermine the importance of new relationships in the spiritual realm. The saying lays the basis for a new spiritual family of God (see Luke 14:26ff.).

The Parable of the Sower, 4:1-20 (Matt. 13:1-23; Luke 8:4-15)

Mark has been described as the Gospel of Jesus' deeds. Such a description is intended to point at Mark's emphasis on Jesus' activities and the way in which these activities, in the Gospel, lead even the modern reader to the conviction that Jesus was the Son of God. As Mark does in fact reflect this sort of emphasis, it is all the more important to take careful notice when he gives attention to other things. In this instance he gives an insight into some of the things that Jesus taught. Even here, however, the underlying interest seems to be in Jesus' activity as a preacher of the kingdom of God.

The Greek word for parable *(parabolē)* seems to depend on the Hebrew word *(mashal)* for its meaning. This term includes a wide range of meanings: "The ethical maxim, the short sentence of popular wisdom, proverbs generally, by-word, taunt-song, oracle, riddle, comparison, allegory, fable, and . . . parable in the strict sense." A number of these uses may be seen in the Gospels. Certainly the parable was one of Jesus' favorite teaching devices, and he used a selection of specific types in a number of ways. He used parables for two basic purposes. First, Jesus used this particular form to convey truth embodied in pictorial language. Second, he might on certain occasions intend by the use

¹ Again he began to teach beside the sea. And a very large crowd gathered about him, so that he got into a boat and sat in it on the sea; and the whole crowd was beside the sea on the land. ² And he taught them many things in parables, and in his teaching he said to them:

---

of parable to stimulate his audience to thought or action, that is, to cause them to apprehend a certain truth. In the former instance for example, one would not soon forget the lesson on forgiveness found in the parable of the prodigal son. In the latter, again by way of illustration, the parable of the good samaritan would have forced his hearers to decide who their "neighbor" was and what their responsibilities were to him.

Although parables may have certain associations with allegory in the New Testament, at least in certain settings, the parables of Jesus are not primarily allegorical in character. In the history of the church there have been many approaches toward the interpretation of Jesus' parables, including the allegorical, but the one that seems to be true in the deepest sense to Jesus' intention is that each parable should be examined for a single basic lesson. If one is interested in the identification of details within the parables, he should look to the explanations of Jesus, a few of which are included in the Gospels. In other instances where such identifications are not made, it is perhaps wise to forego any attempt at such allegorical identification.

[1, 2] The circumstances surrounding Jesus at this particular point in his ministry give a complete and rather intimate background to the nature of the situation. Jesus was teaching **beside the Sea** of Galilee as he often did. His following was growing; there was in fact **a very large crowd gathered about him.** This is one more piece of evidence that in the early days of Jesus' ministry his following grew rather rapidly and reached proportions of considerable size. Such a conclusion is supported by the report that four and five thousand were involved in the two feeding miracles. It was only after Jesus began to speak of the more far-reaching aspects of his ministry that his following began to decrease. At this particular point, however, the crowd was large enough to warrant Jesus' getting in a boat and

³ "Listen! A sower went out to sow. ⁴ And as he sowed, some seed fell along the path, and the birds came and devoured it. ⁵ Other seed fell on rocky ground, where it had not much soil, and immediately it sprang up, since it had no depth of soil; ⁶ and when the sun rose it was scorched, and since it had no root it withered away. ⁷ Other seed fell among thorns and the thorns grew up and choked it, and it yielded no grain. ⁸ And other seeds fell into good soil and brought forth grain, growing up and increasing and yielding thirtyfold and sixtyfold and a hundredfold." ⁹ And he said, "He who has ears to hear, let him hear."

teaching them from the boat as they gathered about the shore, and **he taught them in parables.**

[3-9] In the first parable, the parable of the sower, Jesus described the sower who went out to sow. The man sowed in six different kinds of soil: the path, the rocky ground, the thorny soil, and good soil of three different qualities. Jesus, as he sat in the boat, made no explanation of the various types of soil in which the farmer sowed his seed. If it were not for the solemn injunction at the end, one might conclude that Jesus was simply commenting on the vicissitudes of Palestinian farming. The injunction at the end, **he who has ears to hear, let him hear,** without doubt directs attention to the fact that Jesus was doing something of considerably greater significance. The difficulty of encountering the parable without its explanation is reflected in the fact that later, when the disciples had opportunity, they asked him concerning the meaning of his words.

The parable has been taken by different commentators through the centuries in a number of ways, but the primary emphasis seems to lie on the sower and the seed. At least it is told from that standpoint. The explanation later in the chapter opens up the consideration of the soils into which the seed was sown, but basically the parable was pertinent to those disciples who were to take up the task of sowing. It is not without significance that the same seed in the story yields varying amounts. And, while at first this should be seen as a comment to the disciples about the nature of their task, it also speaks of that with which they were to be working.

[10] And when he was alone, those who were about him with the twelve asked him concerning the parables. [11] And he said to them, "To you has been given the secret of the kingdom of God, but for those outside everything is in parables; [12] so that they may indeed see but not perceive, and may indeed hear but not understand; lest they should turn again, and be forgiven." [13] And he said to them, "Do you not understand this parable? How then will you understand all the parables?

[10-13] Before the interpretation Mark inserts an explanation of the purpose of parables. The statement of Jesus recorded in these verses has presented difficulties to many commentators. As the passage stands, Jesus' purpose in the parables seems to be to make certain things known to those on the inside and to make the same things obscure to those on the outside. Many are troubled that Jesus should care to hide anything concerning the kingdom from outsiders. These persons argue that such would have been directly opposed to Jesus' purpose. Such must be a superficial judgment.

It was a part of Jewish life and culture that parables (riddles) were obscure and that it was the teacher of wisdom who concerned himself with them (*Sirach* 39:1ff.). One could become wise only by attaching himself to such a wise man (*Sirach* 51:23ff.). It was thus only after one had accepted a teacher and his message that the teaching given in parables became understandable.

According to the Gospels, the kingdom is to be seen in the person and work of Jesus. If a man did not accept Jesus, he did not understand his teaching. It was the scribe who had become a disciple to the kingdom who understood the meaning of the parables (Matt. 13:51f.).

The severity of the purpose clause in English, **so that they may indeed see but . . .** , is somewhat modified in observing that it was typical of Hebrew to state the result as a purpose. This may be the situation here (see Isa. 6:9f.). In any case, Jesus was a master at telling stories in such a way that those who wanted to learn could see the lesson, but those who did not could not get a "handle" with which to raise any objection or to accuse him.

¹⁴ The sower sows the word. ¹⁵ And these are the ones along the path, where the word is sown; when they hear, Satan immediately comes and takes away the word which is sown in them. ¹⁶ And these in like manner are the ones sown upon rocky ground, who, when they hear the word, immediately receive it with joy: ¹⁷ and they have no root in themselves, but endure for a while; then, when tribulation or persecution arises on account of the word, immediately they fall away. ᵐ ¹⁸ And others are the ones sown among thorns; they are those who hear the word, ¹⁹ but the cares of the world, and the delight in riches, and the desire for other things, enter in and choke the word, and it proves unfruitful. ²⁰ But those that were sown upon the good soil are the ones who hear the word and accept it and bear fruit, thirtyfold and sixtyfold and a hundredfold.''

ᵐ Or *stumble*

[14-20] Jesus' explanation is well-known and speaks of the different types of individuals within whom the gospel may be "planted." And although it must be recognized as the parable of the "sower," the Markan framework clearly speaks of the "soils."

First, there is the **path** where the seed was taken by the birds; then **the rocky ground** where there was not enough soil for support; and thirdly the ground filled with **thorns** in which the grain could not grow. On the other hand there was the **good soil** of three different qualities. It seems important to stress the fact that there were three different types of good soil, otherwise the parable would be out of balance; surely it is at least equally possible to find good soil as it is to find bad.

Those individuals who represent the **path** are described as being unable to receive the word because of their hardened condition. Consequently, Satan removes the seed. Those characterized as the shallow soil on top of the rock receive the word enthusiastically but, because they have no depth, find **tribulation and persecution** extremely difficult. They **fall away**. Those characterized as among **thorns** are those who let the **cares of the world** enter in and separate them from their faith in Christ. Then there are the good types: one producing thirty times, another

²¹ **And he said to them, "Is a lamp brought in to be put under a bushel, or under a bed, and not on a stand? ²² For there is nothing hid, except to be made manifest; nor is anything secret, except to come to light. ²³ If any man has ears to hear, let him hear."**

sixty, and still another one hundred. One is reminded of the parable of the talents (Matt. 25:14ff.) in which the lesson is quite clear that one is held responsible for the abilities that he has, not for those he does not possess. One should expect people of varying abilities to achieve different things in their work in the kingdom.

The Parable of the Lamp: Measure for Measure, 4:21-25 (cf. Luke 8:16-18)

With regard to the structure of this paragraph, the inclusion of the declaration to hear (vs. 23) seems to indicate that the paragraph contains sayings of Jesus that are not continuous. That is, such language is ordinarily used by the evangelist as a concluding statement. It may be that the two maxims in verses twenty-four and twenty-five are included in the context simply because of their vaguely similar character.

[21-23] In the parable of the **lamp** Jesus suggests the obvious. One would be taken to be a fool if he brought a **lamp** into a room and put it under a cover. This would of course destroy the very purpose of the **lamp.** Yet, apparently Jesus felt that the obvious needed to be stated. He had himself brought the light of the gospel into the world, and the principle he is pointing to is simply that it would be foolish for him to hide the very thing that was supposed to be the reason for his presence. That which had been at least in part hidden—God's plan for the world—was to be made manifest. Indeed it had to be, for God had determined it to be so. In this case the hidden must be brought into the open and the secret brought to the light. Again Jesus' words, **if any man has ears to hear, let him hear,** intone a solemn injunction and somehow in themselves seem to convey a fearful expectation to those who do not give heed.

²⁴ And he said to them, "Take heed what you hear; the measure you give will be the measure you get, and still more will be given you. ²⁵ For to him who has will more be given; and from him who has not, even what he has will be taken away."

---

[24] The phrase **take heed what you hear** must represent Jesus' desire that his disciples acquire genuine spiritual insight. It would appear that it was necessary for them to work at the business of being his followers and that this was not altogether a gift. The more they learned, the more they were in a position to learn; the more they knew, the more they could use what they knew for further learning. And further, Jesus seems to indicate in the last phrase **still more will be given you,** that those disciples who were diligent in their attempt to understand the kingdom would be given even greater insight.

[25] This verse seems to be the briefest sort of allusion to the parable of the talents (Matt. 25:14-30) and continues the preceding thought in a very effective way. Those disciples who persist in pursuing the minimum standard will always discover that their devotion, if it could be so described, will have miserly effects upon them. If one is to follow Jesus, then or now, he must be free in his gift of self. Yet, in that freedom he will realize such continual blessings that he himself will feel that he has not given, but has rather received.

The Parable of Seedtime and Harvest, 4:26-29

This parable is often referred to as the "parable of the seed growing." Such an approach seems to suggest that God somehow works behind the scenes in secret and unknown ways to achieve his purposes in the growth and development of his kingdom. Although there may be a divine relation of this sort to the reality of the kingdom, this parable is better thought of in other ways. The primary emphasis, though admittedly somewhat obscure, seems to lie in urging that harvest—or the ultimate realization of a process—comes naturally, as the culmination of what may be a long series of incidents.

That Jesus' emphasis here is upon harvest seems to be

²⁶ And he said, "The kingdom of God is as if a man should scatter seed upon the ground, ²⁷ and should sleep and rise night and day, and the seed should sprout and grow, he knows not how. ²⁸ The earth produces of itself, first the blade, then the ear, then the full grain in the ear. ²⁹ But when the grain is ripe, at once he puts in the sickle, because the harvest has come."

³⁰ And he said, "With what can we compare the kingdom of God, or what parable shall we use for it? ³¹ It is like a grain of mustard seed, which, when sown upon the ground, is the smallest of all the seeds on earth;

---

indicated in one or two different ways. First there is the reminiscence of Joel 3:13 (vs. 29) where the notion of harvest is developed in some detail. Then too, the same pattern of thought occurs here that is found above (vss. 21f.). There the point of emphasis is that the end result of placing a lamp on a stand is that it might give light. In both of these parables, then, is the idea of a thing being the result or culmination of a series of other things.

[26, 27] Although the idea of culmination is emphasized, there is also in the parable the point that what was being beheld as the kingdom of God was the result of God's doing. Although one may observe things growing, indeed one may plant, water, and reap, yet he is simply coming in touch with God's process at certain points along the way. The process of growth is God's doing, whether in nature or in the kingdom, and man bears his relation to it (see 1 Cor. 3:6).

[28, 29] The primary emphasis, however, does seem to be on the concept of harvest. This alone is justification for calling it the "parable of seedtime and harvest." The parable says that the long period of growth—**blade, ear,** and **full corn**—has been completed; harvest has come. The seed which God planted in Israel many generations past has now come to full fruit and is waiting to be gathered. "The time is fulfilled, and the kingdom of God is at hand; repent, and believe in the gospel" (1:15).

The Parable of the Mustard Seed, 4:30-32 (Matt. 13:31f.; Luke 13:18f.)

[30-32] Although this parable has not always been taken

61

[32] yet when it is sown it grows up and becomes the greatest of all shrubs, and puts forth large branches, so that the birds of the air can make nests in its shade.''

[33] With many such parables he spoke the word to them, as they were able to hear it; [34] he did not speak to them without a parable, but privately to his own disciples he explained everything.

---

to be a lesson concerning the great growth both in size and reputation of the kingdom of God, surely that is its basic message. The picture is drawn of a **grain of mustard seed,** which from small, inconspicuous beginnings (it was popularly regarded in Palestine at the time as the **smallest of all the seeds on earth**) comes to realize itself in a great outgrowth of such a size and glory that the **birds of the air** make their nests in its shade. In retrospect one is left to imagine the lack of adequate projection, even by Jesus' closest followers, of what the kingdom might become.

Jesus' Use of Parables, 4:33, 34 (Matt. 13:34f.)

[33, 34] To the extent that his disciples were capable of comprehending his message, Jesus continued to speak in parables. In fact, it seems to be indicated here that there was at least a period in Jesus' ministry in which he spoke in parables almost exclusively. As one reflects on the nature of the situation, this seems to have come after his following had grown to a size of problematic proportions and before it began to dwindle as a result of his more pointed teaching. The purpose statement here seems to agree with the interpretation of the difficult saying above (vss. 11f.). Jesus did make some explanation of his parables to his disciples, but he did this **privately.** Again one imagines that the parables themselves did communicate truth; yet it was apparently necessary for Jesus to enlarge upon them. As well as explaining specific parables, this enlargement would also have developed an interpretive ability within the disciples.

The Stilling of the Storm, 4:35-41 (Matt. 8:23-27; Luke 8:22-25)

Continuing the observation that Mark's Gospel is often

³⁵ On that day, when evening had come, he said to them, "Let us go across to the other side." ³⁶ And leaving the crowd, they took him with them in the boat, just as he was. And other boats were with him. ³⁷ And a great storm of wind arose, and the waves beat into the boat, so that the boat was already filling. ³⁸ But he was in the stern, asleep on the cushion; and they woke him and said to him, "Teacher, do you not care if we perish?" ³⁹ And he awoke and rebuked the wind, and said to the sea, "Peace! Be still!" And the wind ceased, and there was a great calm.

---

arranged in sections, one notes that here (4:35) another series of miracles begins. The stilling of the storm is followed in chapter five by three of Jesus' most memorable miracles: the Gerasene demoniac, Jairus' daughter, and the woman with the hemorrhage. The cumulative impact of these four narratives is vividly felt in the rejection of Jesus that occurred at Nazareth (6:1-6).

[35, 36] This story of Jesus' influence over the forces of nature is surely one of the most memorable and vivid of all his miracles. Jesus' closest disciples were, of course, men of the Sea of Galilee. They knew it well, and apparently the idea of leaving the crowd appealed to them. Therefore, they set out. Though nothing greater is made of it, the fact that **other boats** went along is also mentioned.

[37] A **storm** arose. The Sea of Galilee is almost seven hundred feet below sea level and severely influenced by its particular location and the surrounding geography. There are a number of fairly sharp descents surrounding the lake which are broken by valleys, particularly the Jordan Valley at the north and again at the south. The nature of this location results in the fact that the lake is extremely subject to winds, which may come up quickly through these breaks between the various descents. Jesus and his disciples were the victims of just such a **wind**.

[38, 39] Jesus was **asleep**; this fact in itself may contain a worthwhile insight into Jesus' humanity. That Jesus was concerned about the size of the crowds has already been mentioned, and it may be that he profited as much as anyone from physical refreshing, here by means of withdrawal and sleep. At any rate, his sleeping became the point of the

⁴⁰ He said to them, "Why are you afraid? Have you no faith?"
⁴¹ And they were filled with awe, and said to one another, "Who
then is this, that even wind and sea obey him?"

---

disciples' concern. They seemed to interpret his unaware-
ness as lack of concern. They became so disturbed that
they woke him with a question implying that he should do
something.

The story has been described as "at once vivid and art-
less." That urgency is expressed is quite clear. The disciples
were concerned for their very lives. The rather brusque
question, **Do you not care if we perish?** is such that the
story may be firsthand. Consistent with the tradition concerning the Gospel, the story probably came from Peter
himself. Vividness is again in Jesus' dramatic command,
Peace! Be still! The order was followed by a great calm.

[40, 41] It is significant that the "breaking in" of the
kingdom of God did not occur only in parables of the kingdom or in miracles of healing. It is significant that here
this so-called "breaking in" is seen in Jesus' control of
nature. As the result of his action, Jesus found a lack of
faith in his followers. The implication seems to be that they
should have had more confidence in God with regard to
the very continuance of life. Apparently they simply could
not restrain themselves and felt it necessary to involve Jesus
in their lack of faith. After the miracle had been performed,
the text says, **they were filled with awe.** They asked, **Who
then is this that even wind and sea obey him?** Whereas they
seemed to have expected him to do something earlier, they
now seem to be overwhelmed by his ability. And, no matter
what the extent of the apprehension of Jesus' being, they
apparently still have much to understand.

Finally, one should contrast the fear that the disciples
had before the storm which Jesus rebuked and the fear mentioned at the conclusion of the Gospel (16:8, see Introduction). There the disciples flee the tomb trembling and astonished for they "were afraid." While there are many things
in life that the disciples of Jesus should not fear because
they were disciples, there is yet the overwhelming fact that
God has acted. There is a legitimate "fear" response to the
awe-inspiring finality of God having become a man.

¹ They came to the other side of the sea, to the country of the Gerasenes.ⁿ ² And when he had come out of the boat, there met him out of the tombs a man with an unclean spirit, ³ who lived among the tombs; and no one could bind him any more, even with a chain; ⁴ for he had often been bound with fetters and chains, but the chains he wrenched apart, and the fetters he broke in pieces; and no one had the strength to subdue him.

ⁿ Other ancient authorities read *Gergesenes,* some *Gadarenes*

Whatever more one might care to make of it, it is quite clear that Jesus is here forcing the question of his own identity. This was the principal way he made himself known (see Introduction). Because of this, the **Who then is this . . . ?** has a relevant quality which has a way of applying itself to modern man.

The Gerasene Demoniac, 5:1-20 (Matt. 8:28-34; Luke 8:26-39)

The second miracle in this series (beginning at 4:35) records the healing of a demoniac and is surely the most vivid as well as the most detailed of all of the demon narratives found in the Gospel (1:23; 3:11). Jesus' incredibly extensive power was openly and dramatically made manifest.

[1] As is indicated in the RSV footnote, the precise name of the place involved in this story is uncertain. There has therefore been a certain amount of speculation with regard to locale. It may have been a Gentile area (see below), and it must have been near the Sea of Galilee.

[2-4] As this story is given in such fullness, a number of insights into the character of demon possession are provided. It might be useful to observe these in some detail. Perhaps the most obvious is that the demoniac led a very strange life. The fact that he **lived among the tombs** may simply indicate that he had been rejected by society and was a public outcast. This point would seem to be confirmed by the fact that it had apparently been impossible to contain him because of his superhuman strength. The experience that different ones had had, at least with this particular demoniac, severely impressed them with his great strength.

⁵ Night and day among the tombs and on the mountains he was always crying out, and bruising himself with stones. ⁶ And when he saw Jesus from afar, he ran and worshiped him; ⁷ and crying out with a loud voice, he said, "What have you to do with me, Jesus, Son of the Most High God? I adjure you by God, do not torment me." ⁸ For he had said to him, "Come out of the man, you unclean spirit!" ⁹ And Jesus° asked him, "What is your name?" He replied, "My name is Legion; for we are many."

o Greek *he*

On close observation it may be seen that Mark used five different phrases to speak of this strength.

[5] The fact that this demoniac was compelled to "cry out" (*krazein*) may also have contributed to his being an outcast. Such behavior would, of course, disturb the normal flow of life wherever it might occur. This deranged person also practiced at least a mild form of self-mutilation, **bruising himself with stones.** Such self destruction is not uncommon among disturbed persons, but in this case it does give a concrete indication of the severity of this particular individual's problem. The figure that is seen after looking at only a few of the characteristics mentioned is striking indeed: a terribly disturbed person, completely disoriented with regard to the realities of life.

[6, 7] Such an extreme disturbance is made all the more remarkable by the observation that despite all his problems, the demon-possessed man recognized Jesus. This recognition led to the openly stated question, **What have you to do with me, Jesus, Son of the Most High God?** It has already been indicated that this is a remarkably regular characteristic of demon possession in the Gospels. Perhaps this is to be understood simply as a graphic example of demons who "believe and shudder" (James 2:19). It is possible to observe a number of different characteristics of modern mentally disturbed individuals that may be paralleled in the text of the Gospels, but nothing is observed comparable to the messianic insight which the demoniacs of the New Testament often possessed.

[8, 9] When asked who he was, the man replied that he was called **Legion.** As a Roman legion, the apparent

¹⁰ And he begged him eagerly not to send them out of the country. ¹¹ Now a great herd of swine was feeding there on the hillside; ¹² and they begged him, "Send us to the swine, let us enter them." ¹³ So he gave them leave. And the unclean spirits came out, and entered the swine; and the herd, numbering about two thousand, rushed down the steep bank into the sea, and were drowned in the sea.

¹⁴ The herdsmen fled, and told it in the city and in the country. And people came to see what it was that had happened. ¹⁵ And they came to Jesus, and saw the demoniac sitting there, clothed and in his right mind, the man who had had the legion; and they were afraid.

---

reference, usually contained between four thousand and six thousand men, there is here an extreme indication of this man's problem. Any sense of his own human identity seems to have been completely obscured.

[10-12] Along with his insight into Jesus' person, the Gerasene demoniac recognized Jesus' power over him. He knew that Jesus could require anything of him he desired. While this is true, it is also interesting to note that the demon felt remarkably free to bargain with Jesus. He did not want to leave **the country** and, as an alternative, begged permission to go into **the swine**.

[13] It would be possible to project a question concerning demons and animals, but no secure conclusion could be reached. And while some have suggested that the **swine** in this story may have destroyed themselves for some other reason, the implication of the passage seems to be that it was because of the demons that the swine plunged themselves into the sea. The final conclusion then may be that it was— at least in this sense—impossible for the demons to dwell in the animals, i.e., that the swine were not able to remain themselves and contain these foreign elements at the same time. If such a suggestion is true, it gives a vivid insight into the severity of demon possession. In any case, the power of Jesus was once again dramatically manifest.

[14, 15] One of the most striking statements about the character of demon possession is found here. Apparently, the extent to which this statement is true of all demon possession may only be a point of conjecture. The temptation

¹⁶And those who had seen it told what had happened to the demoniac and to the swine. ¹⁷And they began to beg Jesus' to depart from their neighborhood. ¹⁸And as he was getting into the boat, the man who had been possessed with demons begged him that he might be with him. ¹⁹But he refused, and said to him, "Go home to your friends, and tell them how much the Lord has done for you, and how he has had mercy on you." ²⁰And he went away and began to proclaim in the Decapolis how much Jesus had done for him; and all men marveled.

p Greek *him*

---

is, of course, to generalize because the description is both modern and intelligible. After the demon was cast out, the man was **sitting, clothed and in his right mind.** Obviously he had formerly been hyperactive, customarily naked, and not "in his right mind." The thought that the man was not in a correct state of mind should not be interpreted in twentieth-century psychological terms. Rather, the attempt must be made to project such a phrase back to the first century. When looking for an adequate definition, the remark about Jesus himself in 3:21 comes to mind. There it is recalled that some of Jesus' friends had come to the opinion that Jesus was "beside himself" *(exestē)*. It is quite clear in the case of the demons that they were recognized by their contemporaries—at least in some sense—as abnormal people. When normality returned after healing, it was quite evident for everyone to see.

It should not be supposed that all demons were the same. Jesus himself seems to have recognized different types (9:29). Sometimes blindness, deafness ("dumbness"), and epilepsy are associated with demon possession (Matt. 9:32-34; 12:22-24; Mark 9:14-29; and parallels). It should be noted that in none of these cases does messianic recognition on the part of the demon-possessed person become a part of the story. The evidence in the Gospels points back to the fact that a certain kind of demon recognized Jesus and that that recognition somehow played an important part in the unfolding drama of Jesus' becoming known to mankind.

[16-20] At least two other elements in this particular story are worthy of note: the possibility of Gentile involve-

²¹ **And when Jesus had crossed again in the boat to the other side, a great crowd gathered about him; and he was beside the sea.** ²² **Then came one of the rulers of the synagogue, Jairus by name; and seeing him, he fell at his feet,** ²³ **and besought him, saying, "My little daughter is at the point of death. Come and lay your hands on her, so that she may be made well, and live."** ²⁴ **And he went with him.**

---

ment, and the commission of the demoniac to his friends. Many have considered the destruction of the swine a problem and have sought a rational explanation, reasoning that Jesus would not have been involved in such an incident. As has been noted, the text is not altogether clear with regard to the cause and effect relationship of the original incident (vs. 13). However, it seems that the destruction of the swine was thought of as the direct result of the activity of the demons. Jews would not in all likelihood have kept swine. The destruction of them here may therefore have been linked with the Jewish attitude toward these animals. This implies that the people involved were not Jewish and may explain to some extent why Jesus told the man who had been possessed to **go . . . tell . . . how much the Lord has done for you,** where in similar contexts elsewhere in the Gospel he usually commanded silence (see *Introduction,* "Messianic Secret"; for *Decapolis,* see Vol. 1, pp. 156ff.). The people concerned reacted negatively to Jesus and begged him to leave, not because they had a similar feeling to that of Peter when he saw the dramatic effectiveness of the Lord's power (Luke 5:8), but because they were full of fear. It would certainly be true that as the man formerly possessed—if he were a Gentile—told his friends and relations about Jesus, there would not be the same reaction as there would be if this story were told among Jews.

Jairus' Daughter and the Woman with the Hemorrhage, 5:21-43 (Matt. 9:18-26; Luke 8:40-56)

The current series of four miracles is made complete by two which are intertwined in such a way that it does them a disservice to separate them. They concern Jairus' daughter and the woman with the hemorrhage.

[21-24a] Jesus had returned apparently to the west side

And a great crowd followed him and thronged about him.
²⁵ And there was a woman who had had a flow of blood for
twelve years, ²⁶ and who had suffered much under many physicians, and had spent all that she had, and was no better
but rather grew worse.

---

of Galilee. A prominent Jew, indeed **one of the rulers of
the synagogue** (see Vol. 1, p. 77), came to Jesus and fell
down before him in worshipful response and with a request.
His whole approach to Jesus concerned **his little daughter**
and reflects the most genuine sort of parental concern. His
request was simple; the condition of his little daughter's
health was very serious, and he asked Jesus simply to **come**
and also to **lay hands** upon her. In such a request he demonstrates a meaningful faith in Jesus' ability to do what he
requested. Jesus' response was immediate and straightforward. One might wonder if Jesus, too, was impressed with
the simplicity of Jairus' faith. Too much comment should
not be made about what is essentially silence, but this story
has traditionally called attention to itself for its open,
unashamed vividness. The simplicity of the relationship
between Jairus and Jesus contributes to this judgment. **Jesus
went with him.**

[24b-26] On the way to Jairus' house, another encounter
took place that directs one's attention aside, at least for
a moment, to others who were deeply concerned about their
problems. In the crowd following Jesus there was a woman
who had been afflicted by some sort of hemorrhage for **twelve
years.** It would be difficult to overestimate the seriousness
of such a condition to the Jewish mind. Not only was there
a depressing physical problem, but such a condition would
also have prohibited this woman's participation, in any full
sense, in the religious rites of Judaism (Lev. 15:25-30). One
can only imagine the seriousness of the woman's reaction
to such a set of circumstances, particularly if she happened
to have been deeply religious. Mark's vividness appears
again in his description of how the woman had **spent all
that she had** and **suffered much** at the hands of **many physicians.** And as a result her condition, instead of becoming
better, had deteriorated.

²⁷ She had heard the reports about Jesus, and came up behind him in the crowd and touched his garment. ²⁸ For she said, "If I touch even his garments, I shall be made well." ²⁹ And immediately the hemorrhage ceased; and she felt in her body that she was healed of her disease. ³⁰ And Jesus, perceiving in himself that power had gone forth from him, immediately turned about in the crowd, and said, "Who touched my garments?" ³¹ And his disciples said to him, "You see the crowd pressing around you, and yet you say, 'Who touched me?' " ³² And he looked around to see who had done it. ³³ But the woman, knowing what had been done to her, came in fear and trembling and fell down before him and told him the whole truth. ³⁴ And he said to her, "Daughter, your faith has made you well; go in peace, and be healed of your disease."

[27-29] The woman **had heard the reports** about Jesus. There is an insight here into the fact that not only was Jesus' popularity growing, there was also a wider awareness of his healing powers. The action of the woman in pressing through the crowd, confident that if she only **touched his garment** she would be made whole, is expressive of her faith (that touching was a normal means of healing, see 6:56). Jesus confirms this at the end of the paragraph (vs. 34) by speaking directly to the woman about her faith. That she was in a state of ceremonial uncleanness makes the act of touching all the more significant. Power flowed forth from Jesus when the woman's faith expressed itself.

[30-34] Jesus knew what had happened. He somehow sensed **that power had gone forth from him. He turned about immediately** to ask the crowd who had touched him. Surely Jesus was not asking for information. As he seems to have done on a number of occasions, he was asking for the benefit of the person involved. The woman, severly impressed and knowing fully that she had been cured by somehow sensing it within herself, **came in fear and trembling.** Further, **she fell down before him and told him the whole truth.** It seems apparent that the woman was deeply touched by the knowledge of two things. On the one hand she had been helped, relieved of the distress of a number of years. And secondly, she could not but be impressed by the power of that person who had healed her. In open response Jesus

71

³⁵ While he was still speaking, there came from the ruler's house some who said, "Your daughter is dead. Why trouble the Teacher any further?" ³⁶ But ignoring ⁴ what they said, Jesus said to the ruler of the synagogue, "Do not fear, only believe." ³⁷ And he allowed no one to follow him except Peter and James and John the brother of James. ³⁸ When they came to the house of the ruler of the synagogue, he saw a tumult, and people weeping and wailing loudly. ³⁹ And when he had entered, he said to them, "Why do you make a tumult and weep? The child is not dead but sleeping."

⁴ Or *overhearing*. Other ancient authorities read *hearing*

relates here the faith of the woman to what had happened and urges her to go in peace.

[35] As Jesus was concluding his remarks to the woman who had been healed, messengers came from Jairus' house reporting that his daughter was dead and suggesting that they not trouble the **teacher** any more. The reference of the messengers to the teacher gives an interesting insight again into the way Jesus was thought of by many of the people. The concept of teacher is, of course, close to that of prophet, with which concept Jesus was most often identified. It is interesting to note that in a context almost completely devoted to healing, Jesus is referred to by this term (see comment on 1:27).

[36-39] Jesus paid no attention to the message of death. His reply to Jairus was simply, **Do not fear, only believe.** And then somewhat curiously, he allows only Peter, James, and John to go with him. As they approach the house, they encounter a crowd, indeed a **tumult,** with considerable lamentation for the deceased. That many of these people were professional mourners, a common practice at the time, seems to be indicated in the fact that their **weeping and wailing** immediately turned to laughter when Jesus suggested that the child was only asleep.

Whether or not Jairus' daughter was actually dead is a question of some interest. The text in Matthew begins by recording the ruler's statement, "My daughter has just died." No mention is made of messengers in the middle of the incident. In all likelihood this is simply Matthew's

72

⁴⁰ **And they laughed at him. But he put them all outside, and took the child's father and mother and those who were with him, and went in where the child was.** ⁴¹ **Taking her by the hand he said to her, "Talitha cumi"; which means, "Little girl, I say to you, arise."** ⁴² **And immediately the girl got up and walked (she was twelve years of age), and they were immediately overcome with amazement.**

---

way of shortening the story. Luke agrees with Mark in recording the fact that messengers came with the word that the girl had died. However, in all three Gospels Jesus urges that the girl was not **dead** but only **sleeping** (vs. 39; cf. Matt. 9:24; Luke 8:52). The essential question here is whether or not Jesus' words should be taken literally. Was the girl simply asleep, that is, presumably in a coma; or should Jesus' expression be taken to mean that she will arise although she is in fact dead? Neither question may appear to be of great importance, as a miracle occurred in either case. The widow's son at Nain (Luke 7:11-17) and Lazarus (John 11) are clear examples of resurrections by Jesus.

[40] Again carrying out the element of mystery, Jesus put **all outside** and took only the father and mother and those with him (presumably Peter, James, and John) **and went in where the child was.**

[41] In the private intimacy of this kind of situation, Jesus took the little girl's hand and said, **Talitha cumi.** Mark's vividness carried this great step further in that he preserves the Aramaic expression (see Introduction). For the convenience of his readers Mark translates, which translation again translated is **Little girl I say to you arise.**

[42a] Mark, with his characteristic **immediately,** emphasizes the fact that the response came quickly. The little girl got up and walked. At this point Mark mentions that **she was twelve years old.** It should be remembered that the woman with the hemorrhage had been in her condition for the same period of time. She, therefore, has been described as a woman "whose misery was as old as Jairus' daughter." It is tempting to speculate on this seeming coincidence. Surely, however, if the woman with the hemorrhage had been Jairus' wife and mother of the girl, it would have been mentioned somewhere in the story.

⁴³ And he strictly charged them that no one should know
this, and told them to give her something to eat.

[42b, 43] Two further points must be mentioned here,
the amazement of the crowd and the charge to silence. Any
attempt to imagine the result of experiencing such an incident
can only lead to a reconsideration of its overwhelming
nature. Surely, no matter how many times one had heard
about or seen Jesus' power, it would have remained impressive. It might be wondered how anyone could resist it. Jesus'
charge to silence has been seen a number of times (see
Introduction, "Messianic Secret"). Obviously, in this case
many people were going to be aware of what had happened
to the girl. Any attempt to hush it up would have met with
highly unlikely success. It seems reasonable to conclude that
somehow these commands fit in with Jesus' plan and that
they were directed ultimately at his own self-revelation. It
is possible that Jesus' ambiguous suggestion that the girl
was asleep was designed for the specific purpose of creating
uncertainty in the minds of those who were not directly
associated with the resurrection. With this, the stage is set
for the rejection at Nazareth.

*The Rejection at Nazareth, 6:1-6a (Matt. 13:53-58; see also
Luke 4:16-30)*

Jesus' summary of this incident, "a prophet is not without honor, except in his own country" (vs. 4), recognizes a
long-standing characteristic of human nature. It has always
been difficult for a great many adults to accept one who
has grown up in their midst. This is to say that such an incident as the one recorded here might have been expected,
especially when Jesus began to project himself in such a way
that it was evident—at least to some— that there was something extraordinary about him.

Considering the elements that make up this situation,
it would not be impossible that such an incident occurred
more than once. There seems to be a definite individuality
to the record of a similar incident in Luke (4:16-30).
There seems to be no common agreement among commentators as to whether the Lukan passage represents a variation

¹He went away from there and came to his own country; and his disciples followed him. ² And on the sabbath he began to teach in the synagogue; and many who heard him were astonished, saying, "Where did this man get all this? What is the wisdom given to him? What mighty works are wrought by his hands! ³ Is not this the carpenter, the son of Mary and brother of James and Joses and Judas and Simon, and are not his sisters here with us?" And they took offense ' at him.

' Or *stumbled*

---

of this same incident or the record of another different but similar encounter.

[1-3] The incident begins with Jesus teaching in the **synagogue**. He seems to be acting in a reasonably well-known and fairly formal role and, up to this point, a role which had not been the occasion of any negative reaction.

When Jesus asserted himself enough to create a strong reaction, the questions came from the people quickly and were penetrating in character: **Where did this man get all this? What is the wisdom given to him? Is not this the carpenter?** And Luke records, "Is not this Joseph's son?" It is clear from these questions that the people of Nazareth expected Jesus, in normal Jewish tradition, to follow in the steps of his father, which he did to some extent. Justin (*Dialogue 88*) speaks of the fact that Jesus made yokes and ploughs. When he began rather to break with this and to reveal himself as something greater, many reactions occurred. In essence, it would appear that the people were simply asking, "Who does he think he is?"

Once again there is an underlying significance to the passage. Mark regularly describes Jesus' miracles as **mighty works** (*dunameis,* cf. 6:5; 9:39 and 5:30; 6:14). He avoids "signs" (*sēmeia*) and "wonders" (*terata*), which are rather to be associated with those who oppose Jesus (cf. 8:11f.; 13:22). Even though astonishment is a regular Markan theme (1:22; 5:20; 6:6; 7:37; 10:24, 26, 32; 11:18; 15:5, 44), faith is the appropriate response to Jesus (6:6). The point is that despite Mark's stress on Jesus' miracles, he does not want to project him as a miracle monger. A miracle must be accompanied by faith (cf. 4:40).

In this connection Jesus' family relationships are brought

⁴ And Jesus said to them, "A prophet is not without honor, except in his own country, and among his own kin, and in his own house." ⁵ And he could do no mighty work there, except that he laid his hands upon a few sick people and healed them. ⁶ And he marveled because of their unbelief. And he went about among the villages teaching.

---

into the open. In addition to Joseph and Mary, his parents, it seems that it was well known that there were brothers and sisters. Four brothers are named, but the fact of sisters is only mentioned in passing. Although this has been a problem to many, there is no reason here to resist the simplest conclusion that these were other children of Joseph and Mary. Epiphanius (about A.D. 380) was one of the first to argue that these were sons of Joseph but not of Mary. Jerome (about the same date) suggested that they were cousins of Jesus, sons of Mary's sister. The motivation behind these later views had to do with protecting the idea of Mary's perpetual virginity. However, the more common non-Catholic view has been that the reality of the virgin birth is in no way endangered by other children being born later to Joseph and Mary. It seems reasonable to conclude that the matter should be left at that.

It should be noted that it is against common Jewish practice for a man to be identified by means of his mother. In fact, identification by means of maternal antecedent at least occasionally carried the overtones of a curse (see Judges 11:1f.). The usual practice was to cite his father. The simplest solution to the question of why it should appear as it does here may be that there seems to have been a rumor circulated very early about Jesus to the effect that he was illegitimate. There is at least a certain amount of biblical evidence of such a charge (see John 8:41; 9:29; etc.).

[4-6] In any case, the people of Nazareth—at least a significant number of them—took this occasion to reject Jesus' new projection of himself. It is then recorded that **Jesus could do no mighty work there.** The people were characterized by unbelief. The idea is not that Jesus was powerless apart from faith, even though verse six mentions **unbelief** (*apistia*). Rather, it would have been foolish for Jesus to demonstrate his power in open defiance of the rejection

⁷ And he called to him the twelve, and began to send them out two by two, and gave them authority over the unclean spirits. ⁸ He charged them to take nothing for their journey except a staff; no bread, no bag, no money in their belts; ⁹ but to wear sandals and not put on two tunics.

---

of the people. Such action would have tended to harden them in their unwillingness to accept him. Whereas Luke records the end result of the incident as being an attempt on Jesus' life, Mark simply states that he went about among the villages teaching.

The Mission of the Twelve, 6:6b-13 (Luke 9:1-6; cf. Matt. 9:35—10:16; Luke 10:1-12)

With the commission of some of Jesus' disciples to go out and accomplish a certain task, the ministry of Jesus moved into a new era. He was no longer a teacher without a following or without a certain recognition. Apparently considerable teaching had taken place and it was therefore felt that his followers were ready. There can be no doubt also that Jesus had in mind a testing, an opportunity for his disciples to get the feel of their own abilities. This was a factor with considerable ramifications if one considers the power they were given not only over disease but also over the forces of evil. One should not overlook the fact, however, that Jesus was also concerned that the disciples gain some practical experience. It is clear that the mission of these disciples was an extension of the ministry of Jesus. Here one sees the symbolic significance of the *twelve*: Jesus is not gathering a remnant but calling all Israel.

[7] The fact that Jesus sent his disciples out **two by two** indicates that there was a certain practicality about the association and that it was not simply an ideal circumstance. They were given **authority over the unclean spirits,** that is, they shared the same power exercised by Jesus. Again the character of Jesus' ministry as a deliberate confrontation with the sources of evil is manifest.

[8, 9] Jesus gave his disciples explicit instructions with regard to the limited amount of preparation they should make. They were to take **no bread, no bag, no money,** not

77

[10] And he said to them, "Where you enter a house, stay there until you leave the place. [11] And if any place will not receive you and they refuse to hear you, when you leave, shake off the dust that is on your feet for a testimony against them." [12] So they went out and preached that men should repent. [13] And they cast out many demons, and anointed with oil many that were sick and healed them.

---

even a change of clothing (**tunics,** the short-sleeved, knee-length undergarment). They were to wear **sandals** and carry a **staff** (in Luke a staff is also forbidden; in Matthew both staff and sandals are among the excluded items). It has been suggested that the variation in the accounts at this point is the result of the fact that travelers wore different things in different parts of the empire. In this case, the discrepancy may represent an attempt to adjust the story to the various cultural practices of those to whom the specific Gospel was written. Apparently these instructions were designed not only as a means of testing the quality of the disciples but also the sincerity of those who were to receive them. Their physical needs would have been obvious and the response to those needs was to be an indication of the receptivity of those with whom they came in contact.

[10, 11] Where they were received, they were to go in and stay. The length of their stay was to be dependent upon the kind of reception they received. If there was a lack of receptivity within a given household, the disciples were instructed to leave and look for another place where their message might be more acceptable. So severe was this element in their commission that Jesus instructed them that when they left an unreceptive house they were to demonstrate their attitude by the solemn Jewish custom of shaking off **the dust** of their **feet for a testimony against them,** i.e., that they were heathen and that the missionary responsibility of the disciples had been fulfilled toward them (cf. Acts 13:51; 18:6).

[12, 13] The disciples followed Jesus' instructions. They went out and preached repentance. The indication is, of course, that their message was identical—at this stage—with that of John (see Matt. 3:2; Mark 1:4) as well as of Jesus himself (see Mark 1:15). Their power over the **demons** was

78

¹⁴ King Herod heard of it; for Jesus'ʼ name had become known. Some ʼ said, "John the baptizer has been raised from the dead; that is why these powers are at work in him." ¹⁵ But others said, "It is Elijah." And others said, "It is a prophet, like one of the prophets of old."

ˢ Greek *his*
ᶠ Other ancient authorities read *he*

---

made known; **they cast out many.** The **sick** were also the object of their attention and received healing as well. Again such activity accords with that of Jesus. For **oil** in the care of the sick see Isaiah 1:6; James 5:14; Luke 10:34.

Mark thus gives the matter-of-fact account of one early commission to Jesus' disciples. Later (see vs. 30), when the disciples had accomplished their mission, they returned to report to Jesus what they "had done and taught."

Jesus' Fame—The Murder of John the Baptist, 6:14-29 (Matt. 14:1-12; Luke 9:7-9)

By this time in his ministry Jesus was the object of considerable attention, and it appears that many were interested in him in one way or another. These popular reactions to Jesus are significant in that they give an insight into the way in which Jesus was received. When Jesus began to press those issues that were most central and were to have the greatest effects, many of this popular following turned away from him (see John 6). As this sort of change became part of the situation, it seems that Jesus—withdrawing to some degree himself—began to concentrate more and more on teaching his disciples and arranging for them to have those experiences which would enable them to accomplish their longer-ranged mission.

[14, 15] Technically, **Herod** Antipas (see Vol. 1, p. 60) was not a **king** but a "tetrarch," yet Mark follows popular usage. The three reactions to Jesus listed here are preparatory to Peter's confession (8:27ff.). The reaction of some was that John the Baptist had been **raised from the dead.** This seems to have been a fairly popular opinion and may have been based on Herod's fear mentioned later in the paragraph. Others had concluded that in Jesus they had

79

¹⁶ But when Herod heard of it he said, "John, whom I beheaded, has been raised." ¹⁷ For Herod had sent and seized John, and bound him in prison for the sake of Herodias, his brother Philip's wife; because he had married her. ¹⁸ For John said to Herod, "It is not lawful for you to have your brother's wife." ¹⁹ And Herodias had a grudge against him, and wanted to kill him. But she could not, ²⁰ for Herod feared John, knowing that he was a righteous and holy man, and kept him safe. When he heard him, he was much perplexed; and yet he heard him gladly.

---

found the long-awaited reappearance of **Elijah.** Malachi 4:5 suggests that Elijah was to return to herald the advent of the Messiah. Apparently this passage had not yet been linked with the appearance of John the Baptist. Such a link was later established (see Matt. 17:9-13) and the meaning of Malachi was clarified. Others, slightly more vague, suggested that Jesus was a prophet like one of the prophets of old. It was natural that Jesus should have been so identified. He often preached against the evils that he saw within his society and in this did identify himself with the prophetic tradition. An eschatological prophet was expected to herald the last days.

[16-20] The conviction that John the Baptist had been raised from the dead, as has been indicated, may have been dependent in some measure upon Herod's fear. Yet one might query the rationale for the identification inasmuch as the ministries of the two men overlapped. It is at least possible that Antipas may not have heard of Jesus, since at the beginning of his ministry Jesus was not as prominent as John. Then too, their ministries had been separate geographically: Jesus in Galilee, John in Samaria and Perea (1:5; 3:7f.).

Herod had taken his brother Philip's wife, **Herodias,** as his own, and John had spoken openly against this action which broke Jewish law (Lev. 18:16; 20:21). The **Philip** of the passage is not to be confused with the ruler of Ituraea (Luke 3:1) who later married Salome. John's rebuke of the illicit marriage had particularly stung Herodias. She was Jewish and was therefore justly subject to Jewish law. Antipas' mother was a Samaritan, which may have made the

²¹ But an opportunity came when Herod on his birthday gave a banquet for his courtiers and officers and the leading men of Galilee. ²² For when Herodias' daughter came in and danced, she pleased Herod and his guests; and the king said to the girl, "Ask me for whatever you wish, and I will grant it." ²³ And he vowed to her, "Whatever you ask me, I will give you, even half of my kingdom." ²⁴ And she went out, and said to her mother, "What shall I ask?" And she said, "The head of John the baptizer."

---

rebuke slightly less direct toward him. In any case, Herodias clearly appears as a conniving woman determined to have her own way regardless of cost. When she set herself against John, Herod felt concerned to act and yet shows his own character by not doing all his wife desired. Herod was content to confine John in prison, whereas Herodias wanted him killed. Herod's inclination to protect John seems to have been based on his understanding that there was something special about him. Indeed, Herod possessed a certain fear of John, **knowing that he was a righteous and holy man.** In addition, the insight is given that although he was disturbed by it, he was intrigued by what John had to say.

[21-23] Herod gave a feast on his birthday for all of the officers and officials near him as well as the leaders within the province. At this feast Salome (Josephus gives the name) performed. The dance that she gave was obviously very pleasing and Herod promised her a gift to the **half** of his **kingdom.** The statement, which may sound rash, was conventional (1 Kings 13:8; Esther 5:3, 6; 7:2; Luke 19:8).

[24] Popular tradition has usually interpreted Salome's dance to have been one filled with sexual provocation. In this connection it has been sometimes referred to as the "dance of the seven veils." However, it has recently been suggested that Salome may have been quite young (ten or twelve) and that the response that she received from Herod was rather based on her innocence and childhood purity. Two thoughts may contribute to such a radical change in interpretation of this passage. First, it may not have been likely that Herod's own step-daughter would have danced a provocative type of dance, especially before this audience. Surely, even the Roman authorities would have drawn some lines. Secondly, the fact that the girl went

²⁵ And she came in immediately with haste to the king, and asked, saying, "I want you to give me at once the head of John the Baptist on a platter." ²⁶ And the king was exceedingly sorry; but because of his oaths and his guests he did not want to break his word to her. ²⁷ And immediately the king sent a soldier of the guard and gave orders to bring his head. He went and beheaded him in prison, ²⁸ and brought his head on a platter, and gave it to the girl; and the girl gave it to her mother. ²⁹ When his disciples heard of it, they came and took his body, and laid it in a tomb.

³⁰ The apostles returned to Jesus, and told him all that they had done and taught. ³¹ And he said to them, "Come away by yourselves to a lonely place, and rest a while." For many were coming and going, and they had no leisure even to eat. ³² And they went away in the boat to a lonely place by themselves. ³³ Now many saw them going, and knew them, and they ran there on foot from all the towns, and got there ahead of them.

---

out to consult her mother in regard to what she should ask may indicate that she was not mature enough to make her own decisions. It appears that the facts contained in the paragraph are not sufficient to decide between these alternatives.

[25-29] Salome returned to the king's presence quickly at the suggestion of her mother to ask for the head of John the Baptist. Herod was **exceedingly sorry.** Yet, he had made his **oath** before his **guests** and his honor manifested itself in such a way that it was impossible for him to refuse, yet, on reflection, a refusal might have been taken as an indication of even greater stature. But because of his reactions, he gave orders for John's **head** to be brought. He then gave it to Herodias. The recalling of the incident concludes with the simple but somber mention of the fact that John's disciples made it their task to bury the body.

The Feeding of the Five Thousand, 6:30-44 (Matt. 14:13-21; Luke 9:10-17; cf. John 6:1-14)

[30-33] This important incident in the life of Jesus began when his disciples returned from their preaching tour in which they had made some significant preparation for the coming kingdom. The text clearly implies that they

³⁴ **As he went ashore he saw a great throng, and he had compassion on them, because they were like sheep without a shepherd; and he began to teach them many things.** ³⁵ **And when it grew late, his disciples came to him and said, "This is a lonely place, and the hour is late;** ³⁶ **send them away, to go into the country and villages round about and buy themselves something to eat."**

---

showed signs of weariness and fatigue. Jesus therefore suggested that they find a place where they could rest awhile. The place where they were was so busy that it was not convenient to eat. They got into the boat and set out for a lonely place where they might refresh themselves. But they found it impossible to get away from the crowd. While they were going by boat, many others found their way round about by land and, in fact, were even waiting for Jesus when he arrived.

[34] This verse contains two important keys to the understanding of the circumstance. First, the people who gathered themselves around Jesus **like sheep** are described as being **without a shepherd** (Num. 27:17; 1 Kings 22:17; Ezek. 34:5). This extremely descriptive analogy may not be meaningful to those who know only urban life. Sheep are essentially "dumb"; they lack any great ability to help themselves, and they will follow one another for no reason, without purpose, and with no concern about where they may be going. Perhaps when the analogy is drawn with people, a better word might be "helpless." The people following Jesus apparently did not have the ability to help themselves. He was offering them something of himself. They may not have understood completely, but they knew that they were receiving something from him and, therefore, they wanted more. They were helpless, sensing some need but unable to satisfy themselves.

The second key lies in the fact that Jesus **had compassion upon them** because he was sensitive to these needs. He could not avoid responding when their desperate condition was so evident. If Jesus had not felt the way he did about these followers, nothing more would have happened. The remainder of the story is dependent upon his **compassion**. He, therefore, took the opportunity to teach them.

[35, 36] His disciples reflected a practical concern. They

³⁷But he answered them, "You give them something to eat." And they said to him, "Shall we go and buy two hundred denarii " worth of bread, and give it to them to eat?" ³⁸And he said to them, "How many loaves have you? Go and see." And when they had found out, they said, "Five, and two fish." ³⁹Then he commanded them all to sit down by companies upon the green grass. ⁴⁰So they sat down in groups, by hundreds and by fifties.

" The denarius was a day's wage for a laborer

---

realized that the time was getting away and that there was not enough food available for the people, so they suggested that the teaching be terminated in order to give the people time to find themselves something to eat.

[37, 38] Jesus' response may indicate that he already had a plan in mind. He suggested to his disciples that they feed the crowd. Their response is one of bewilderment. The only possibility they could apparently envision was that they should go and buy large amounts of bread and bring it back for the people. Efforts to give a monetary equivalent for ancient money are misleading. The denarius was the standard Roman silver coin and represented the daily wages of a soldier and common laborer (Matt. 20:2). Jesus sent them to discover how much food they had already in their possession. In an extremely direct command he said, **Go and see.** They discovered **five** loaves and **two fish,** hardly enough even to begin with such a large crowd.

[39, 40] Mark's description of the nature of the situation has attracted the attention of scholars through the ages. The observation is regularly made that he is here at his best with regard to vivid detail. Mark's Gospel is known in its entirety for the fact that it contains detailed descriptive elements (see Introduction). Often, in the other Gospels, there is hardly enough for the reader to see the detail of the original situation.

Jesus commanded the people to sit down in groups. They sat **upon the green grass** in groups **of hundreds and fifties.** With the preparation complete, the distribution was ready to begin.

⁴¹**And taking the five loaves and the two fish he looked up to heaven, and blessed, and broke the loaves, and gave them to the disciples to set before the people; and he divided the two fish among them all.** ⁴²**And they all ate and were satisfied.** ⁴³**And they took up twelve baskets full of broken pieces and of the fish.** ⁴⁴**And those who are the loaves were five thousand men.**

[41-44] Jesus **looked to heaven** and **blessed** the food and in turn gave it to his disciples, who were to give it to the people. The terminology closely approximates the last supper (14:22). Either the incident has been retold to bring out its anticipations of the Lord's Supper, or the actions of Jesus were familiar things which he then endowed with new significance in the last supper. Bread and fish are regularly present in the symbolic representations of the Lord's Supper in early Christian art. The text says **they all ate and were satisfied.** In fact, there was substantially more food left over than there was in the beginning. The word for **basket** *(kophinos)* is a container commonly carried by Jews to keep from having to buy bread from Gentiles. In the story of the feeding of the four thousand the word is *spuris,* a much larger basket, big enough to hold a man (Matt. 15:37; Mark 8:8). The whole incident becomes all the more impressive when the reader discovers at the end that there were **five thousand men** present, not to speak of women and children.

On the basis of the text as it stands in Mark, one might wonder whether or not the people realized that something extraordinary was happening. There is no indication whatsoever of any response on their part. Is it possible that they were not aware of the miracle?

Later (vs. 52) the text reflects that Jesus' disciples **did not understand about the loaves** and that **their hearts were hardened.** Surely it was a difficult set of circumstances to comprehend. Five loaves and two fish, yet everyone was satisfied and ample left over. What happened? For the eye that had never seen such an incident, certainly bewilderment would have been a natural reaction.

The suggestion that **their hearts were hardened** probably should not be taken to mean that they were somehow divine-

⁴⁵Immediately he made his disciples get into the boat and go before him to the other side, to Bethsaida, while he dismissed the crowd. ⁴⁶And after he had taken leave of them, he went up on the mountain to pray. ⁴⁷And when evening came, the boat was out on the sea, and he was alone on the land. ⁴⁸And he saw that they were making headway painfully, for the wind was against them. And about the fourth watch of the night he came to them, walking on the sea. He meant to pass by them,

---

ly prohibited from understanding. It should rather be taken as evidence of the fact that they did not understand. If one's mind had suddenly received such fantastic data, it would be extremely difficult to appropriate the facts immediately.

Walking on the Water, 6:45-52 (Matt. 14:22-33; cf. John 6:15-21)

[45] Mark begins this incident by revealing that **Jesus made his disciples go to the other side** of the sea. No reason is given in Mark why Jesus should have treated them in this way. If one compares the account in John (see 6:15), the reason becomes clear. There it is recorded that Jesus felt the people were at the point of forcefully making him king. Withdrawal and reconsideration were therefore necessary. One is always faced with the difficulty of understanding just how Jesus could do what he came to do in fulfilling God's plan without the sincere but unthoughtful actions of others getting in the way. No doubt his commands to silence often involved his own awareness that if things got "out of hand" in the wrong way, he would not be able to accomplish his purposes. When it became apparent that the crowd would have desired to force Jesus into an earthly kingship, he found it necessary simply to avoid the circumstances in which such might occur.

[46] The fact that Jesus separated himself and went into the hills **to pray** must give an insight into his nature. It should not be supposed that Jesus understood his final destiny and purpose from the moment of his birth; rather, just the opposite is implied. When he separated himself to pray, one should consider the possibility of open communication

⁴⁹ but when they saw him walking on the sea, they thought it was a ghost, and cried out; ⁵⁰ for they all saw him, and were terrified. But immediately he spoke to them and said, "Take heart, it is I; have no fear." ⁵¹ And he got into the boat with them and the wind ceased. And they were utterly astounded, ⁵² for they did not understand about the loaves, but their hearts were hardened.

---

between Jesus and his Father. The few simple insights that the Gospels give into Jesus' relation with his Father make it possible to conclude that it was a beautiful one and that there was the deepest of meaningful relationships between them, even during Jesus' earthly ministry.

[47, 48] The disciples had gone ahead of Jesus, and he was to follow. Later in the evening, when they were out in the boat, he saw that they were having difficulty in **rowing.** The **wind was against them** and it was apparently impossible for them to accomplish their goal. The division of the night into four watches was Roman; the time would have been just before dawn. It seems to be implied that Jesus initially went to help them, but it is later recorded that he intended to pass by them, apparently without offering assistance.

[49-52] He was **walking** on the water and they, thinking they saw a **ghost,** were frightened. The fact that they were distressed caused Jesus to turn to them, mainly, it would appear, to quieten their fears. As opposed to a similar incident in chapter four (vss. 35-41) where Jesus commanded the elements, here his very presence brought about a calm. This, linked with the disciples' lack of understanding about the miraculous feeding of the five thousand, caused another and perhaps even deeper consternation. Mark summarizes: **they were utterly astounded.**

In the account in Matthew (14:28-31), a memorable incident involving Peter is recorded that is omitted from this account in Mark. Peter asked the Lord to bid him to walk on the water too. In making his attempt, Peter could not manage to keep his attention on the Lord. Fear arose within him because of the wind, and he began to sink. Jesus reached out to save him. Mark's omission of such a personally embarrassing event may somewhat corroborate the tradition that this Gospel was closely associated with Peter.

 ⁵³ And when they had crossed over, they came to land at Gennesaret, and moored to the shore. ⁵⁴ And when they got out of the boat, immediately the people recognized him, ⁵⁵ and ran about the whole neighborhood and began to bring sick people on their pallets to any place where they heard he was. ⁵⁶ And wherever he came, in villages, cities, or country, they laid the sick in the market places, and besought him that they might touch even the fringe of his garment; and as many as touched it were made well.

¹ Now when the Pharisees gathered together to him, with some of the scribes, who had come from Jerusalem, ² they saw that some of his disciples ate with hands defiled, that is, unwashed. ³ (For the Pharisees, and all the Jews, do not eat unless they wash their hands,ᵛ observing the tradition of the elders; ⁴ and when they come from the market place, they do not eat unless they purifyʷ themselves;ᵃ and there are many other traditions which they observe, the washing of cups and pots and vessels of bronze.ˣ''

ᵛ One Greek word is of uncertain meaning and is not translated
ʷ Other ancient authorities read *baptize*
ᵃ Other ancient authorities read *and they do not eat anything from the market unless they purify it*
ˣ Other ancient authorities add *and beds*

Healing at Gennesaret, 6:53-56 (Matt. 14:34-36)

[53-56] The chapter concludes with a general statement of healing which occurred when they arrived at **Gennesaret.** They apparently missed Bethsaida, which was their original destination (see vs. 45). Jesus' popularity is still increasing; people act simply on the basis of recognizing him. A certain amount of organization in gathering the sick to Jesus may be implied (vs. 55). The people knew Jesus as a healer and, in their desperation, brought their sick that they might have even the slightest opportunity of being made well. So severe was their motivation that they hoped even for a **touch** of his clothing. Their desires were not unrewarded.

Concerning Cleanliness, 7:1-23 (Matt. 15:1-20)

[1-4] The fact that Jesus, in the process of the development of his ministry, became more widely known is evi-

⁵ And the Pharisees and the scribes asked him, "Why do your disciples not live ʸ according to the tradition of the elders, but eat with hands defiled?" ⁶ And he said to them, "Well did Isaiah prophesy of you hypocrites, as it is written,
'This people honors me with their lips,
but their heart is far from me;
⁷ in vain do they worship me,
teaching as doctrines the precepts of men.'
⁸ You leave the commandment of God, and hold fast the tradition of men."

ʸ Greek *walk*

---

denced again here. Some of the scribes came all the way from Jerusalem to observe him and the things that he did. It is apparent that their motivation was not altogether pure. They observed that at least some of his disciples did not follow the ritual washings. The evidence indicates that there were many washings of various sorts that had grown up in the Jewish tradition. The text indicates that **all Jews** (not to be taken literally, of course) washed before eating and that they did not eat without purifying themselves if they had been to the **market place.** In addition to these specific items, Mark also makes reference to **many other traditions.** In texts of this type, one must always be careful to distinguish between references to the law which meant in one way or another Old Testament scripture, and **tradition** which was thought of as "oral law," consisting in the main of directives relating to specific situations as to how to implement the instruction of scripture. It was these later impositions that Jesus usually condemned.

[5-8] On the basis of their observation, the Pharisees and the scribes approached Jesus questioning why his disciples did not observe the **tradition of the elders.** Without answering their question, Jesus countered with an objection to their hypocrisy. The citation is from the Septuagint of Isaiah 29:13 and was used to accuse the Pharisees and their companions of being **hypocrites.** Jesus saw clearly the hearts of many who went through the motions of a cetain religious observance, but with whom that observance was an end within itself. Jesus, understandably, would have men to be truly religious in their hearts. He summarizes their wrong

⁹ And he said to them, "You have a fine way of rejecting the commandment of God, in order to keep your tradition! ¹⁰ For Moses said, 'Honor your father and your mother'; and, 'He who speaks evil of father or mother, let him surely die'; ¹¹ but you say, 'If a man tells his father or his mother, What you would have gained from me is Corban' (that is, given to God)ᶻ— ¹² then you no longer permit him to do anything for his father or mother, ¹³ thus making void the word of God through your tradition which you hand on. And many such things you do."

ᶻ Or *an offering*

---

attitude here by saying, **You leave the commandment of God, and hold fast the tradition of men.**

[9-13] Jesus was not content to leave the situation without going into greater detail. He continues by giving a specific example. The fifth of the ten commandments urged that honor be given to **father and mother,** and if one did not comply with this command he should **die.** Jesus reminds the Jews of this by quoting the command in full. He then proceeds to show them that the traditions which they had allowed to grow up resulted in an open disregard for the fifth commandment. According to this tradition, anything could be declared **Corban.** The technical meaning of the root word is "offering" or "oblation"; the root verb form means "to bring near" and was used to speak of offerings made to God. Apparently at this time the calling of the formula **Corban** over a given object did not mean that it was inevitably taken into religious use. The indication is that a Jew could say in effect, "That is **Corban** to you." If said to one's **father** or **mother,** it meant that the item in question could not be used by them, but it did not necessarily mean that it had to go for religious purposes. In this way what could have been a perfectly good tradition was used as a means of avoiding a genuine application of the law itself. This is what Jesus meant when he suggested that the tradition was in fact preventing a genuine observance of the law. It would seem highly unlikely that any of the scribes or rabbis would have upheld such a view, but the implication is that at least some of them did. Jesus, however, was not content to stop here either.

[14] And he called the people to him again, and said to them, "Hear me, all of you, and understand: [15] there is nothing outside a man which by going into him can defile him; but the things which come out of a man are what defile him."[a] [17] And when he had entered the house, and left the people, his disciples asked him about the parable. [18] And he said to them, "Then are you also without understanding? Do you not see that whatever goes into a man from outside cannot defile him, [19] since it enters, not his heart but his stomach, and so passes on?"[b] (Thus he declared all foods clean.) [20] And he said, "What comes out of a man is what defiles a man. [21] For from within, out of the heart of man, come evil thoughts, fornication, theft, murder, adultery, [22] coveting, wickedness, deceit, licentiousness, envy, slander, pride, foolishness.

[a] Other ancient authorities add verse 16, *"If any man has ears to hear, let him hear"*
[b] Or *is evacuated*

[14-16] At this point, Jesus began to elaborate upon what he meant by using yet another example, again within the structure of ritual law. The Jews had a complex system of food laws, partly given in the Old Testament, but mostly arising out of their oral tradition. These dietary laws were of great consequence in the life of the early church (Acts 10:9ff.; Gal. 2:1ff.; Rom. 14:1ff.). They taught that there were many things a man should not eat because such would defile him. Jesus, in typical fashion, saw through the intent of the law at this point and urged that there was **nothing** that could go into a man that would defile him. Rather, it was what came out that was important.

[17] The teaching was apparently left at this point, and the scene shifts into the house. When it was possible, the disciples asked what he meant. Jesus then enlarged upon the terse **parable.**

[18-22] Nothing from the outside going into a man could defile him because, Jesus said, it would not go into his **heart** but rather into his **stomach** and ultimately be passed on. This statement occasioned the comment of the Gospel writer, which may have originated as a later realization, that this statement of Jesus made **all foods clean.** Jesus urged the point that it was that which came out of the man that defiled

²³ **All these evil things come from within, and they defile a man."**

---

him. It is within a man's heart, Jesus said, that his basest evils originate. That is, it is within the reflective part of man's nature that he cultivates evil thoughts. Out of this quiet cultivation come **evil thoughts, fornication, theft, murder, adultery, coveting, wickedness, deceit, licentiousness, envy, slander, pride, foolishness.**

It is uncommon to find "vice lists" in the teaching of Jesus, although such lists appear in texts dating both before and after the period in which he lived. The list in this passage has a definite Old Testament character (see Cranfield), and reminds one of similar lists that are found in Paul (e.g., Col. 3:5ff.).

[23] It was within this kind of psychological religious revolution that Jesus most clearly demonstrated his insight into human nature. From a practical point of view, in terms of things that affect human existence, these are some of the most important teachings of Jesus. **All these evil things come from within, and they defile a man.**

The Demon Possessed Child, 7:24-30 (Matt. 15:21-28)

If Mark's Gospel should be examined for the movements of Jesus from place to place, one would be impressed by the fact that the bulk of Jesus' life was spent in the region of Galilee with the occasional mention of other places, both within (Nazareth, Cana) and without (Caesarea Philippi, Decapolis) that general area. Ultimately, of course, Jesus' movement toward Jerusalem and the fulfillment of his purpose there enter in and these more provincial incidents fall away. A significant interruption to the fundamental simplicity just mentioned is found here when Jesus visited the coastal region of Phoenicia, well above Galilee and to the west.

It has often been suggested that Jesus may have made this trip to avoid the hostility of Herod. While this may be true, the record of this incident does not seem to be placed as it is in Mark to explain that situation. It rather records a significant encounter between Jesus and

²⁴ And from there he arose and went away to the region of **Tyre and Sidon.**ᶜ And he entered a house, and would not have any one know it; yet he could not be hid. ²⁵ But immediately a woman, **whose little daughter was possessed by an unclean spirit,** heard of him, and came and fell down at his feet. ²⁶ Now the woman was a Greek, a Syropheonician by birth. And she begged him to cast the demon out of her daughter. ²⁷ And he said to her, **"Let the children first be fed, for it is not right to take the children's bread and throw it to the dogs."** ²⁸ But she answered him, **"Yes, Lord; yet even the dogs under the table eat the children's crumbs."**

ᶜ Other ancient authorities omit *and Sidon*

---

a foreigner. With few exceptions the subjects of Jesus' healing and teaching were his own people. Exceptions to such extablished generalities always merit attention. If one assumes in this case that Jesus' approach to a foreigner was significant, one could conclude that Jesus was laying a foundation for later developments toward the Gentiles. Indeed, more or less, this entire chapter, both in subjects discussed and places visited, seems to be held together by the interests of Gentile Christianity. The clarity of this particular woman's worthiness could serve as an argument for the inclusion of others in the kingdom of God.

[24-26] Jesus was trying to avoid being found and went to **Tyre and Sidon.** Although he was away from his normal environment, he was recognized, in this case by a woman **whose little daughter was possessed by an unclean spirit.** Expressing a parental concern, she came to Jesus, **fell down at his feet,** and **begged** for help.

[27, 28] Jesus' response is problematic and somewhat difficult to understand. It has been said that he addressed the woman "with a smile." One can make such a conclusion only by reading into the present text. Jesus said to the woman, **Let the children first be fed, for it is not right to take the children's bread and throw it to the dogs. Children** here refers to Israel (see Matthew), the **dogs** are foreigners (according to Jewish usage) like the woman to whom Jesus is speaking. If the statement is taken at face value, one would expect it to be offensive to the woman. Her response

²⁹ And he said to her, "For this saying you may go your way; the demon has left your daughter." ³⁰ And she went home, and found the child lying in bed, and the demon gone.

³¹ Then he returned from the region of Tyre, and went through Sidon to the Sea of Galilee, through the region of the Decapolis. ³² And they brought to him a man who was deaf and had an impediment in his speech; and they besought him to lay his hand upon him.

---

being so immediate and clever seems to indicate that Jesus was by his statement creating a situation in which the woman might show her depth and faith. True, Jesus' ministry was first addressed to Jews, and Gentiles were only secondarily recipients of the blessings of the kingdom of God. The woman, in her answer, admits this. **Yes, Lord; yet even the dogs under the table eat the children's crumbs.** In this statement she recognized the selection of Israel as God's chosen; yet she would beg for the remains that in the figure were being wasted.

[29] The healing occurred. Mark records the reason as **For this saying.** Matthew calls attention to the faith of the woman.

[30] The healing took place at a distance (see Matt. 8:5-13; Luke 7:1-10; John 4:46-53). It is a fact, though somewhat unusual, that Jesus occasionally did heal at a distance. Such an incident makes a detailed narrative like the healing of Jairus' daughter (ch. 5) all the more significant for its concern with the journey to the place where the incident was to occur. One concludes that when Jesus went to great lengths to prepare a certain situation for a given individual or individuals, it must have been significant.

A Deaf Man, 7:31-37 (Matt. 15:29-31)

[31, 32] This transitional incident begins by recording the fact that when Jesus returned from Tyre and Sidon he went through **Decapolis.** There is no indication of the time span in the verse, but it may have been weeks if not months. In this circuitous journey he encountered a deaf man who, though able to speak, could not do so correctly. A request came to Jesus to help him.

³³ And taking him aside from the multitude privately, he put his fingers into his ears, and he spat and touched his tongue; ³⁴ and looking up to heaven, he sighed, and said to him, "Ephphatha," that is, "Be opened." ³⁵ And his ears were opened, his tongue was released, and he spoke plainly. ³⁶ And he charged them to tell no one; but the more he charged them, the more zealously they proclaimed it. ³⁷ And they were astonished beyond measure, saying, "He has done all things well; he even makes the deaf hear and the dumb speak."

¹ In those days, when again a great crowd had gathered and they had nothing to eat, he called his disciples to him, and said to them,

---

[33-37] Jesus took the man **aside**. This fact is stressed in such a way that one concludes that this healing was performed in private. Jesus **put his fingers into his ears** and **touched his tongue.** Many have interpreted this as a sort of communication by means of signs. The very fact that Jesus took him **aside** may imply that communication was difficult. Special measures were therefore necessary for Jesus to make himself understood. Jesus' manipulation of the man's ears and tongue is obviously related to the fact that these organs were the object of his attention. Jesus' prayer is expressed by looking into heaven and sighing, again indications of a kind of language that could be understood by the man being healed. Then Jesus said **Ephphatha,** an Aramaic expression Mark interprets as **be opened**. The healing was accomplished; his ears were opened, and his tongue released. He could hear and express himself normally.

Then follows the charge to secrecy which has been given a number of times (see Introduction, "Messianic Secret"). Those concerned, however, would not comply with Jesus' request. Indeed Mark tells us that the more Jesus asked, the more they told the story. Mark records their reaction as astonishment **beyond measure.** Jesus did everything **well,** they observed, even making the **deaf hear** and the **dumb speak.**

The Feeding of the Four Thousand, 8:1-10 (Matt. 15:32-39)

[1-5] As the developments in Jesus' ministry move steadily — even methodically — toward the climax of the confes-

² "I have compassion on the crowd, because they have been with me now three days, and have nothing to eat; ³ and if I send them away hungry to their homes, they will faint on the way; and some of them have come a long way." ⁴ And his disciples answered him, "How can one feed these men with bread here in the desert?" ⁵ And he asked them, "How many loaves have you?" They said, "Seven." ⁶ And he commanded the crowd to sit down on the ground; and he took the seven loaves, and having given thanks he broke them and gave them to his disciples to set before the people; and they set them before the crowd. ⁷ And they had a few small fish; and having blessed them, he commanded that these also should be set before them. ⁸ And they ate, and were satisfied; and they took up the broken pieces left over, seven baskets full. ⁹ And there were about four thousand people. ¹⁰ And he sent them away; and immediately he got into the boat with his disciples, and went to the district of Dalmanutha. *ᵈ*

ᵈ Other ancient authorities read *Magadan* or *Magdala*

---

sion (8:27ff.), Jesus is cast a second time in the role of feeding a multitude. And once again he is motivated by his own **compassion.** The crowd had been with him for **three days** and had **nothing to eat.** This is one more penetrating insight into the feelings of those who followed Jesus across the countryside. For a sizeable group of people to go **three days** without food, even on Jewish reckoning, indicates their strong complusion to be with him, whatever the personal cost. Jesus had the power to send them away, but his **compassion** for them prohibited his doing so without giving them something to eat. He apparently observed certain things which indicated that some of them would not be able to make the journey to their homes without food. Such a specific and detailed indication of Jesus' concern for the welfare of his followers must also be an index by which to evaluate his concern for their spiritual well-being.

[6-10] The crowd was told to sit down. Jesus, in a way similar to the earlier story, took the **loaves,** gave thanks, and handed them to the disciples, who in turn distributed them among the people. The same action is repeated with the **few small fish.** After the excess food was gathered up, Jesus sent them away, which indicates that although great

[11] The Pharisees came and began to argue with him, seeking from him a sign from heaven, to test him. [12] And he sighed deeply in his spirit, and said, "Why does this generation seek a sign? Truly, I say to you, no sign shall be given this generation." [13] And he left them, and getting into the boat again he departed to the other side.

---

crowds followed Jesus, he did have control over them. The story concludes by saying that Jesus went with his disciples to a place called **Dalmanutha.** Matthew mentions "Magadan." As the former is unknown, the location is sometimes associated with Magdala near Tiberias on the west side of the lake. Although the narrative ends rather abruptly, the incident sets the stage for Jesus' teaching later in the chapter (8:14-21).

The Demand for a Sign, 8:11-13 (Matt. 16:1, 4; cf. Matt. 12:28f.; Luke 11:16, 29; 12:54-56)

[11] As was typical, the Pharisees proceed to demand a sign *(sēmeion)* from Jesus **to test him.** Apparently they wanted some open and final proof that he was God incarnate. The "mighty works" *(dunameis,* see comments on 6:1ff.) of Jesus were not intended to dazzle. Even here it is unlikely that this is the request being made. The issue rather had to do with what way Jesus fulfilled a more apocalyptic kind of speculation. Associations with Jonah in other similar situations (see below) seem to point in such a direction.

As is indicated in the parallel references, this was not the only time that Jesus was put to this particular test. One common answer to this demand was to inform the people that they would finally be made aware of "the sign of Jonah" (Matt. 16:4; Luke 11:29). In this figure Jesus found a meaningful way to express his ultimate act. The primary point seems to have been that, as the great fish finally gave up Jonah, so would the earth yield up Jesus. It may well be also that the comparable time factor contributed to the desirability of the model.

[12, 13] Jesus was, of course, disturbed by such an approach. Typical of Markan insight into the emotions of Jesus, the text says he **sighed deeply.** Such must point toward

¹⁴ **Now they had forgotten to bring bread; and they had only one loaf with them in the boat.** ¹⁵ **And he cautioned them, saying, "Take heed, beware of the leaven of the Pharisees and the leaven of Herod."**^c ¹⁶ **And they discussed it with one another, saying, "We have no bread."**

^c Other ancient authorities read *the Herodians*

---

the anguish of heart Jesus experienced when he encountered those who did not even understand themselves, much less him. He so longed for the people to understand his purpose, but many did not. Understanding that they would be no nearer genuine conviction if he overwhelmed them according to their requests, he flatly refused. In this case even an allusion to Jonah is omitted. Rather, he simply **left.**

Bread and Belief, 8:14-21 (Matt. 16:5-12; cf. Luke 12:1)

[14, 16] The section begins by stating the fact that the disciples had neglected to make adequate preparation for the trip. When they realized what they had done, they observed in the simplest terms, **we have no bread.** Here again one is puzzled by the dedication and devotion of the disciples on the one hand and their apparent contradictory lack of understanding that Jesus would provide for their physical needs on the other. In this context Jesus seems to have been motivated by a similar observation.

[15] Considerable discussion has arisen with regard to whether or not verse fifteen should be included in this context. Some (e.g., Hunter) have held that it does not properly belong but was added because of the similarity of subject matter. Others (e.g., Cranfield) feel that it does belong, but that the principle suggested in it simply did not come into the subsequent discussion (cf. Matthew). In either case the statement is a memorable one from Jesus, specifically indicating his view of the Pharisees.

When Jesus suggests that his followers should beware of the leaven of the Pharisees and Herod, he is primarily concerned about their influence. The figure of leaven is used several times in the New Testament to convey something bad (cf. 1 Cor. 5:6-8; Gal. 5:9). Such a usage may be dependent to some extent upon the fact that the rabbis used the

[17] And being aware of it, Jesus said to them, "Why do you discuss the fact that you have no bread? Do you not yet perceive or understand? Are your hearts hardened? [18] Having eyes do you not see, and having ears do you not hear? And do you not remember? [19] When I broke the five loaves for the five thousand, how many baskets full of broken pieces did you take up?" They said to him, "Twelve." [20] "And the seven for the four thousand, how many baskets full of broken pieces did you take up?" And they said to him, "Seven." [21] And he said to them, "Do you not yet understand?"

term to speak of the evil disposition in man. It is used clearly with good intention only in Matthew 13:33 (see Luke 13:21). Again it is strange (see 3:6) that the Pharisees should be linked with Herod. One can only envision people of such diverse backgrounds and purposes being joined together by a strong common purpose. Matthew at this point mentions Pharisees and Sadducees which would present quite another picture.

[17-21] Jesus reacted with a flat question as to why they should be concerned because they forgot bread. In this he questioned their perception and understanding. The feeling is left that he was somewhat disturbed by their lack of comprehension and by their inability or perhaps unwillingness to give themselves completely into his service and let him concern himself with their needs. He couched such a feeling in the penetrating question, **Are your hearts hardened?** He suggested that they have both eyes and ears with which to see and hear and memories with which to recall. He then reviewed the two incidents in which he met needs exactly like those of the present situation. He asked them about the **five thousand** who were fed and how much was left over; the **four thousand** and again what was left. He forced them to answer but then again sadly concluded by asking, **Do you not yet understand?**

The Blind Man of Bethsaida, 8:22-26

A significant number of commentators have concluded that this incident is a duplication of the one found in 7:31ff. Indeed there are a number of significant similarities, yet

²² **And they came to Bethsaida. And some people brought to him a blind man, and begged him to touch him. ²³ And he took the blind man by the hand, and led him out of the village; and when he had spit on his eyes and laid his hands upon him, he asked him, "Do you see anything?" ²⁴ And he looked up and said, "I see men; but they look like trees, walking." ²⁵ Then again he laid his hands upon his eyes; and he looked intently and was restored, and saw everything clearly. ²⁶ And he sent him away to his home, saying, "Do not even enter the village."**

the striking fact that this miracle took place in two steps must stamp this narrative as unique and therefore not a duplication of the earlier incident.

[22-24] Bethsaida here is probably Bethsaida Julias, a village on the north of the Sea of Galilee a mile or so removed from the lake itself in a setting in itself inspirational. The blind man was brought to Jesus by a group of people apparently concerned with the man's welfare. Their concern is expressed in the fact that they **begged** Jesus to help him. There was, of course, a certain expression of faith in such a request. Jesus took the man out of the village. Some have suggested that he did this for the sake of privacy.

Jesus approached a cure by putting spittle upon the man's eyes. Some commentators suggest that such was generally thought at that time to be effective, but it is difficult to verify such a claim. Jesus then followed with a question, **Do you see anything?** And then follows the unique reply from the man that he did see, but that **men** appeared as **trees**.

No other narrative concerning Jesus' ministry records such an incident. Everywhere else Jesus' cures are effective, complete, and often immediate. Why this one should be uniquely different remains something of a mystery. Was there some purpose in a two-step miracle? Could it be that the incident in its way prepares the way for the succeeding paragraph where two levels of understanding are one of the points of concern? That is, to see Jesus as a prophet is not in itself wrong but grossly inadequate. Is therefore viewing Jesus as a prophet comparable to seeing men as trees? Unfortunately, conformation does not come easily to such an interpretation. However, that the incident was

²⁷ **And Jesus went on with his disciples, to the villages of Caesarea Philippi; and on the way he asked his disciples, "Who do men say that I am?"**

---

puzzling even in the first century may be confirmed by its omission from both Matthew and Luke.

[25, 26] Jesus, by means of a second application of his hands upon the man's eyes, completed the healing. Mark makes this emphatic by saying that the man **saw everything clearly.** The incident concludes when Jesus sent the man home, warning him to avoid even going back into the **village.** Prepared or not, the reader is at this point on the threshold of dramatic developments.

THE WAY TO JERUSALEM, 8:27—10:52

Messiahship and Suffering, 8:27-33 (Matt. 16:13-23; Luke 9:18-22)

This incident, which includes Peter's confession, is the turning point of the Gospel. The secret of messiahship emerges finally and completely. But messiahship means suffering, the thing which had apparently not been anticipated by any of Jesus' followers. This element became so important that it is fair to characterize discipleship in terms of participation in suffering. That is, to follow Christ means to share one way or another in his suffering.

[27] The scene is **Caesarea Philippi**, a remote beauty spot some twenty-five miles north of Bethsaida, the last town mentioned. Herod Philip rebuilt and renamed the city after the Roman Emperor. The city should not be confused with Caesarea on the coast of Palestine where Paul was imprisoned.

It is obvious that the disciples' understanding of Jesus was crucial to any progress toward the establishment of a fellowship bearing his name. It was therefore necessary that the great christological question should come sooner or later. Jesus had, for a fairly lengthy period, attempted to impress them with the life he lived. That, of course, was the first means of communicating his identity. But for a true acceptance of Messiah to develop in the minds of even his closest followers, it was necessary for him to press

101

²⁸ **And they told him, "John the Baptist; and others say, Elijah; and others one of the prophets."**

---

them. Here, as it shall be seen, Jesus pressured his disciples to understand and accept the fact that he was to suffer. This must have been a significant addition to their comprehension at this point. In any case, Jesus began by asking, **Who do men say that I am**?

[28] Jesus' question provoked a three-pronged answer. In this answer it is possible to see three important contemporary feelings or reactions to Jesus (cf. 6:14f.).

The association between Jesus and John the Baptist may have been linked to Herod's fear (again see 6:14ff.). Against his own better judgment, Herod had been responsible for John's death. The text in the earlier incident implies that Herod, because of his guilt, developed a rather strange expectation that he might somewhere subsequently encounter John.

There may also have been a more natural link. Both John and Jesus followed in the same prophetic tradition. As John spoke out against the evils of his time, so did Jesus. They would have impressed their contemporaries as the same basic type men. It is apparent, then, that the connection may have been established in more than one way.

The coming of **Elijah** was also a part of current Jewish expectation. Malachi 4:5, 6, which is the closing paragraph of the Old Testament, served as the background for this insertion into the Jewish tradition. Consequently, a preparatory figure came to be expected. (For the link — or absence of it—between Elijah and John see comments on 9:11-13.)

Continuing to pursue the association with prophetic figures, the third portion of the disciples' reply suggests that some thought Jesus was simply **one of the prophets.** Surely the evidence leads to the conclusion that this was the most common positive reaction to Jesus during this ministry and quite understandable when one remembers that the ministry appeared after a fashion common to many of the Old Testament prophetic ministries. In the Old Testament the prophets are regularly found as real men, deeply committed to God, who saw evils in the religious and social orders of their day which they could not resist condemning.

²⁹ **And he asked them, "But who do you say that I am?"
Peter answered him, "You are the Christ."** ³⁰ **And he charged
them to tell no one about him.**

³¹ **And he began to teach them that the Son of man must
suffer many things, and be rejected by the elders and the
chief priests and the scribes, and be killed, and after three
days rise again.**

Because of this, one comes to define an Old Testament
prophet as "God's man speaking against the evils of the
establishment." It might be further added that these answers
were current messianic expectations that were applied to
outstanding men (cf. John 1:19).

[29] Jesus' first question, along with the replies, set the
stage for the second, **But who do you say that I am?** Peter
openly and directly replied, **You are the Christ.** In such an
answer the primary recognition is that of messiahship. In
Peter's answer, Matthew adds, "the Son of the living God."
Luke records Peter's answer as, "the Christ of God."

Messiahship was therefore at this point a realized fact,
however inadequately it may have been conceived. From
a literary point of view this is the first time open mention
was made of it. It is impossible to know whether Peter's
reply actually reflects a concept that he had perhaps enter-
tained for some time or whether Christ's direct question
elicited his final decision. That is, one wonders whether
Jesus forced the issue in this way with a question, or whether
the disciples came to their own individual conclusion.
Matthew speaks of the realization of messiahship as the
revelation of God (Matt. 16:17).

[30] Once more, recognition is followed by a command
to silence. The following verses show Jesus' distinctive
understanding of the meaning of messiahship.

[31] Immediately following the open recognition of messiahship, Jesus introduced the necessity of suffering. Without exception the predictions of suffering occur in all three
synoptic Gospels after Peter's confession. Again, Jesus'
death is not important until his identity is made clear. That
is, if he had not been the Son of God, his death would
have held no special ultimate meaning for man. Thus in
Mark's allocation of space, the new disclosure of the mean-

³² **And he said this plainly. And Peter took him, and began to rebuke him.** ³³ **But turning and seeing his disciples, he rebuked Peter, and said, "Get behind me, Satan! For you are not on the side of God, but of men."**

---

ing of messiahship is more important than the confession of messiahship.

This immediate insistence upon the meaning of Jesus' messiahship may also serve another purpose, i.e., a redirection of popular expectation. Inasmuch as Messiah (Christ) had been conceived more in terms of a politically oriented savior, there would have been a compelling need for Jesus to correct such a view.

The phrasing of verse thirty-one is therefore extremely significant: **And he began to teach them that the Son of man must suffer. . . .** It was at this point that suffering was first mentioned. Only after Jesus was recognized did he speak of suffering. And significantly, Jesus spoke not only of suffering but also of rejection, death, and resurrection. The first prediction of suffering is, therefore, quite inclusive.

[32] The text emphasizes that Jesus said this **plainly.** That is, he left no doubt about the matter. Peter, in response to the suggestion, **took him and began to rebuke him.** This must be understood as simply the reaction of a friend. Peter was, at least at first, reluctant to accept the notion that Jesus must suffer. This is one example of what is meant when it is said that Peter's conception of messiah was "inadequate." Although Peter recognized Jesus as Messiah, he did not yet fully understand what this meant. Later (14:31), Peter said, "If I must die with you, I will not deny you." Deny, of course, he did, but nevertheless his acceptance of the meaning of messiahship had obviously made considerable progress.

[33] The text indicates that before Jesus responded to Peter's rebuke, he looked at his disciples. Such may indicate that Jesus' response to Peter was influenced by the fact that Jesus saw agreement with the sentiments expressed by Peter on the faces of his other followers. Because the situation demanded a strong response, Jesus said severely, **Get behind me Satan.** He accused any who were not sym-

pathetic with the necessity of suffering of being on the **side of men.** He wanted them to be on the **side of God.** This was not easy. It has always been difficult to understand how there could ever have been strength in suffering or why the whole emergence and growth of Christ's church was established upon such a phenomenon. Surely the slowest understanding to come to Jesus' earliest followers had to do with how victory could be found in death. Yet the death of Jesus was the one most necessary thing in the climactic emergence of God's purpose.

Even in view of these generalities, the precise point of the passage must not be overlooked. Jesus' rebuke sharply accused Peter of wanting God's messianic agent to conform to his own conception. Compare Matthew 4:10 where Jesus addresses "begone" (*hupage,* the same word recorded here addressed to Peter) to Satan after he had tempted Jesus with a political kingdom. Jesus thus insists that if one is truly to be his disciple, one must be made into his image, hence the discussion on the nature and cost of discipleship that follows.

There is yet another, more subtle point being made here. After Peter's confession, Jesus' correction of the understanding of the confession, and then Peter's rejection of it, one might expect an explicit discussion of Jesus' messiahship. Instead Jesus offered a discussion of discipleship in terms which relate the disciple to the suffering Lord. It is as if Mark is saying that Jesus' identity is not a matter for speculation or rationalization (see again Matt. 16:17). Jesus can be truly known only as one follows him.

The Nature of Discipleship, 8:34—9:1 (Matt. 16:24-28; Luke 9:23-27)

It is clearly evident that the turning point of Mark's Gospel is to be found in the recognition of Jesus as the Messiah. Upon the basis of that recognition, Jesus began to teach his followers that the way of suffering was to be his way. This was met with a complete lack of understanding. As has been mentioned, the disciples found it extremely difficult to comprehend how glory should ever be found in such humiliation. It was therefore necessary for Jesus

³⁴ And he called to him the multitude with his disciples, and said to them, "If any man would come after me, let him deny himself and take up his cross and follow me. ³⁵ For whoever would save his life will lose it; and whoever loses his life for my sake and the gospel's will save it. ³⁶ For what does it profit a man, to gain the whole world and forfeit his life? ³⁷ For what can a man give in return for his life?

---

to teach his followers about discipleship. They must go the way of their Master.

[34] The first principle of discipleship, according to Jesus, was self-denial. As Jesus suffered, so also would his followers suffer. If one would follow Jesus, he must set his own personal interests aside. Then he must **take up his cross and follow**(see Matt. 10:38). A view of discipleship is sometimes projected that seems to say that if one is not suffering physically because of following Jesus that he is not really Jesus' follower. Suffering may indeed be necessary, but it is not found as a part of every follower's discipleship. To deny one's own personal interests means to put Jesus first. But physical suffering is not an inevitable part of discipleship.

[35] This saying merits careful attention. The phrase, **whoever would save his life** (*psuchē*, "soul," see Matt. 12:39) speaks of that person who would be selfish with himself, his time, and abilities for his own purposes. The person who is selfish with his own life, who lives for his own selfish purposes, will **lose his life. Lose,** in this context, must mean something like "damn." That is, that person who thinks he can use his own human existence for his own purposes will find himself eternally damned. Such is fundamental to the most basic teaching of Christ (see 10:45; cf. 2 Cor. 4:5).

On the other hand, that person who gives his life for the sake of Jesus and the gospel, will **save** it. One may have his life eternally only by giving it away temporally. One might be led to speculate that even this kind of a giving up is in itself a joyous self-satisfying thing. While this may be true, Jesus himself does not seem to go quite this far in the passage at hand.

[36, 37] These verses point out simply but dramatically that there is no price that a person can set as a value for

³⁸For whoever is ashamed of me and of my words in this adulterous and sinful generation, of him will the Son of man also be ashamed, when he comes in the glory of his Father with the holy angels.''

¹And he said to them, "Truly, I say to you, there are some standing here who will not taste death before they see that the kingdom of God has come with power."

---

his **life** *(psuchē)*. As far as physical human existence and material possessions are concerned, all men value them; yet, when one views eternity, all of the wealth of the world cannot be compared to the value of a single individual spiritual eternity.

[38] Many aspects of Jesus' teaching are included in this cluster of sayings. At this point Jesus speaks of his role as mediator between the **Father** and man. Jesus quite happily represents man to the Father, but here he urges that he does not do so in any wrong proportion. As one represents Jesus in this **adulterous and sinful generation,** so will he be represented by Jesus before the Father (Matt. 10:32f.). Note the Old Testament use of adultery in the religious sense of unfaithfulness to God (Jer. 3:8; Ezek. 23:34; Hos. 2:2-10).

[1] The concluding paragraph of chapter eight extends into chapter nine. Jesus promises here that even some of those who were present with him would **see that the kingdom of God has come with power.** The use of **taste** for experience is common (in reference to **death,** cf. John 8:52; Heb. 2:9).

There has been lengthy discussion as to the specific reference Jesus is making. A favorite object of speculation has been the manifestation of divine **power** on Pentecost (Acts 2). One should note, however, that the very next paragraph concerns the transfiguration which, of course, was also a great manifestation of divine power. If Jesus' own life may in any sense be considered as the "breaking-in" of the kingdom of God, then Jesus' reference here may indeed be to the transfiguration. Then too, there is the possibility that Jesus is not referring to any one specific incident but rather to a series of incidents. In this case, the transfiguration may be considered simply one in a series of manifestations of power ultimately leading to the establishment of the Christian commu-

² And after six days Jesus took with him Peter and James and John, and led them up a high mountain apart by themselves;

---

nity (Acts 2; note also the associations of power with the resurrection, Eph. 1:19f.; Rom. 1:4, and the coming of the Holy Spirit, Luke 24:49; Acts 1:8). At the same time, however, one should not forget that there were many other manifestations of **power** even after Pentecost.

The Transfiguration, 9:2-8 (Matt. 17:1-8; Luke 9:28-36)

There were a few points in Jesus' life where something quite out of the ordinary happened to him. Such instances are Jesus' baptism, the transfiguration, and the crucifixion with its attendant glorification. The distinguishing fact is that these events mainly involve divine action directed toward Jesus and do not consist, as do the healing miracles, of action initiated by Jesus. If nothing else, this fact alone places them in a special category.

The exact nature of Jesus' appearance, though described in some detail, still remains elusive. The entire incident is one of those things that always carries the impact felt whenever the divine intrudes into the human. Whenever this happens, even the believing man must stand in awe. He sees something; he knows that something has happened. He is inclined to look toward the divine; yet at the same time he remains largely ignorant. The reality of his own existence may become more vivid, but the reality of the divine unknown remains the more dominating factor.

[2a] It is a well-known fact that **Peter, James, and John** were in some sort of preferred position with Jesus (cf. 5:37; 14:33). A number of times in the course of the ministry these three are drawn into incidents in a way that the others are not. It is quite unlikely that Jesus made any formal distinction between his disciples. Yet there were differences. In all likelihood, any distinction that was recognized would have been so on the basis of inherent ability.

Again a mountain becomes important in the Jewish-Christian tradition. Such had, of course, been a part of the heritage of Judaism since Sinai (Ex. 24:13, 33). The imagery

and he was transfigured before them, ³and his garments
became glistening, intensely white, as no fuller on earth could
bleach them. ⁴And there appeared to them Elijah with Moses;
and they were talking to Jesus. ⁵And Peter said to Jesus,
"Master,ʃ it is well that we are here; let us make three booths,
one for you and one for Moses and one for Elijah." ⁶For he
did not know what to say, for they were exceedingly afraid.

ʃ Or *Rabbi*

---

of the total situation described in this passage consists of
a reasonably clear allusion to the days in the wilderness
and the events of the first Exodus.

[2b, 3] In this incident Jesus was **transfigured** *(meta-
morphein)*. That is to say, his form, or perhaps the appearance of his form, was altered. It is fruitless to make any more
specific interpretation of this change within Jesus other than
that made in the text itself. Mark speaks in detail of the
change in Jesus' clothing; they were **glistening, intensely
white.** They were whiter than it was humanly possible to
make them. (A **fuller** was one who rubbed "fuller's earth"—
a kind of white clay—into the stains on a garment that they
might not be seen.) Both Matthew and Luke, in addition to
the mention of the change in the clothing, add that Jesus'
"face" or "appearance" *(prosōpon)* was also transformed.

[4-6] The next marvel in this sequence consists in the
appearance of Elijah and Moses who were conversing with
Jesus. What is the meaning of the presence of these two
great Old Testament characters? Do they represent the law
and the prophets? It may be that association was intended
between this incident and the Jewish tradition that these
two men had been translated (2 Esdras 6:26). As far as
the New Testament is concerned, the significance of the
event may be seen in the Lukan addition (9:31f.) and Peter's
discussion (2 Peter 1:16-18).

Luke explicitly balances the eschatological glory evident
in the transfiguration with the passion (cf. also 9:22). He
is in fact saying that the death of Christ is necessary. Peter's
desire to build booths is an expression of his ignorance (Luke
9:33). He has not yet understood the necessity of the cross.
Mark emphasizes Peter's fear and makes it the reason for
his uncertainty as to what to say. Luke clearly relates the

⁷ **And a cloud overshadowed them, and a voice came out of the cloud, "This is my beloved Son;ᵍ listen to him." ⁸ And suddenly looking around they no longer saw any one with them but Jesus only.**

ᵍ Or *my Son, my* (or *the*) *Beloved*

---

transfiguration to Christ's death (*exodos,* see 9:31). In 2 Peter 1, the fact that Peter witnessed the transfiguration is made the reason for his confidence that his readers will have full knowledge after his (i.e., Peter's) death (again, *exodos,* 2 Peter 1:15), the "putting off of his body" (tent, booth, *skēnas,* vs. 14). The application is, of course, different, and specific consequences are drawn for the later church from the event. But the point is that Peter's death is near, as had been that of Christ (cf. 2 Peter 1:13 with 1:16), and that eventually the disciples will come to fuller understanding.

The question of the nature and development of Jesus' own self-understanding is one that perennially troubles scholars. It seems only logical that the awareness within Jesus was similar to that in other human beings. This of course is not always evident. There may be implied in the very fact of this discussion the idea that Jesus only gradually became aware of the nature of his purpose and the ultimate personal sacrifice that would eventually be required of him. Somehow the notion of omniscience must be reconciled with the fact that Jesus was incarnate in a human body. This is simply one form of the problem one always encounters in attempting to comprehend the incarnation.

[7] The next incident in the sequence is the divine blessing, again reminiscent of the baptism. The heavenly voice announced, **this is my beloved Son; listen to him.** The addition of the phrase **listen to him** (cf. 1:11) from Deuteronomy 18:15 ("the prophecy of the messianic prophet") is significant. The entire incident made "the prophetic word more sure" (2 Peter 1:19). It is striking that Jesus remained silent during the transfiguration. **Listen to him** therefore draws attention to the sayings in the context (8:31—9:13) concerning suffering, resurrection, and the imminence of the kingdom.

[8] According to the text, the vision (Matt. 17:9) came to an abrupt end. The disciples looked around and saw no one, except Jesus.

⁹ And as they were coming down the mountain, he charged them to tell no one what they had seen, until the Son of man should have risen from the dead. ¹⁰ So they kept the matter to themselves, questioning what the rising from the dead meant. ¹¹ And they asked him, "Why do the scribes say that first Elijah must come?" ¹² And he said to them, "Elijah does come first to restore all things; and how is it written of the Son of man, that he should suffer many things and be treated with contempt? ¹³ But I tell you that Elijah has come, and they did to him whatever they pleased, as it is written of him."

The Question about Elijah and John the Baptist, 9:9-13 (Matt. 17:9-13; cf. 11:7-14)

[9] After the deep impressions of the transfiguration, Jesus once again charged his disciples to be silent about what they had seen (see Introduction, "Messianic Secret"). Here Jesus openly anticipates the resurrection. He speaks of himself once again in terms of the **Son of man.** The association of glorification with the Son of man theme is common. In his own way Jesus gave an amazingly complete indication all through his ministry of things to come with regard to himself. The fact that Jesus gave such indications always makes one wonder why his followers did not more clearly understand his purpose and the ways in which his purpose was to be effected.

[10] The preceding observations are established in the fact that although the disciples were willing to keep quiet about what they had seen and heard, they still did not accept the necessity of Jesus' death. This has a curious ring of penetrating insight. They wanted to be obedient, but they did not understand. Indeed, they were willing to obey but their questionings still remained, as surely they would to most when the concept of resurrection was introduced.

[11-13] Apparently the Jewish tradition had attached great significance to the prophecy of Malachi (esp. 4:5, 6). The disciples raised their question about it at this point —and in this context—because they still had not understood the nature of Jesus' messiahship. It is quite clear that they were expecting Jesus to strike a pose similar to that of Elijah, as John had done (cf. Matt. 11:3, "the coming one," and

¹⁴ And when they came to the disciples, they saw a great crowd about them, and scribes arguing with them. ¹⁵ And immediately all the crowd, when they saw him, were greatly amazed, and ran up to him and greeted him. ¹⁶ And he asked them, "What are you discussing with them?" ¹⁷ And one of the crowd answered him, "Teacher, I brought my son to you, for he has a dumb spirit; ¹⁸ and wherever it seizes him, it dashes him down; and he foams and grinds his teeth and becomes rigid; and I asked your disciples to cast it out, and they were not able." ¹⁹ And he answered them, "O faithless generation, how long am I to be with you? How long am I to bear with you? Bring him to me." ²⁰ And they brought the boy to him; and when the spirit saw him, immediately it convulsed the boy, and he fell on the ground and rolled about, foaming at the mouth. ²¹ And Jesus ʰ asked his father, "How long has he had this?" And he said, "From childhood.

ʰ Greek *he*

Mal. 3:2). Messiah was in fact to be God's forerunner before the "day of the Lord" (see Mal. 3:1; 4:5). Christ's talk of death and resurrection painted quite another picture than that which had been expected. Matthew adds, "Then the disciples understood that he was speaking to them of John the Baptist" (Matt. 17:13; cf. 11:14). The prophecy of Malachi had been fulfilled. Elijah (John the Baptist) had come and the way was open for the appearance of Messiah. And even though the disciples still seem to lack anything like complete understanding (see e.g., 9:30-32), there had been some development in their comprehension.

The Epileptic Boy, 9:14-29 (Matt. 17:14-21; Luke 9:37-43a)

In this story of a boy and his father, there is an impressive manifestation of faith as well as weakness in the context of human problems. Nevertheless, the richness of the passage is evident in a number of ways.

[14-21] The terminology associated with this incident is somewhat unusual. Mark mentions a **dumb spirit** (*alalos,* vs. 17), a **spirit** (vs. 20), and a **dumb and deaf spirit** (*alalos, kōphos,* vs. 25); Matthew only mentions "demon" (*daimonios,* 17:18); Luke has "spirit" (9:39), "demon" (*daimonios,* 9:42), and "unclean spirit" (*akathortos,* 9:42).

²² **And it has often cast him into the fire and into the water, to destroy him; but if you can do anything, have pity on us and help us." ²³ And Jesus said to him, "If you can! All things are possible to him who believes." ²⁴ Immediately the father of the child cried out and** ' **said, "I believe; help my unbelief!"**

' Other ancient authorities add *with tears*

Matthew records the father as saying that his son was an "epileptic" (*selēniazetai*, i.e., "moonstruck," 17:15). The verb may be translated "epileptic" here because of the descriptions of the symptoms. The boy was deeply troubled by severe seizures (vs. 18). All three accounts explain this in considerable detail. Mark's addition of **dumb and deaf** (vs. 25) points up other factors. Perhaps it should be observed that the boy possessed many sources of difficulty. During this time it seems to have been common to attribute various types of physical difficulties to demon possession. It should be obvious because of this that the term "demon" in the various Gospel narratives may mean a number of different things, mainly bound up with what were otherwise inexplicable human problems.

The boy's father had asked the disciples for help, but they were not able to give it. It appears that when Jesus approached the crowd it was already evident that the disciples were not going to be able to fulfill the father's request. There seems to be a significant amount of discussion at the expense of the boy. The fact that there was a discussion between the father and the disciples, followed by the one between the father and Jesus, might be taken to indicate that the boy was being neglected, time was being wasted. When the healing did occur, it happened so quickly that Matthew inserts the word "instantly."

The most impressive part of Mark's account of this incident concerns the father's encounter with Jesus. In the process the father reflected some sort of faith. It may have been simply a confidence in Jesus' healing power. Surely it was more than that. Even though the father had made some achievement with regard to his faith, the pressure of this situation caused him to reflect the need for even greater.

[22-24] After the father and Jesus had discussed the situa-

113

²⁵ And when Jesus saw that a crowd came running together, he rebuked the unclean spirit, saying to it, "You dumb and deaf spirit, I command you, come out of him, and never enter him again." ²⁶ And after crying out and convulsing him terribly, it came out, and the boy was like a corpse; so that most of them said, "He is dead." ²⁷ But Jesus took him by the hand and lifted him up, and he arose. ²⁸ And when he had entered the house, his disciples asked him privately, "Why could we not cast it out?" ²⁹ And he said to them, "This kind cannot be driven out by anything but prayer."ʲ

ʲ Other ancient authorities add *and fasting*

tion in some detail, the father simply said, **If you can do anything . . . help us.** Jesus seems almost to be offended by the phrase, **If you can!** After repeating the words apparently with great emphasis, Jesus said, **All things are possible to him who believes.** Thus, Jesus himself openly introduced the subject of faith, and the father was cast in a situation which seemed to him to require an open and emphatic declaration of his own faith. He cried out, **"I believe; help my unbelief!"**

[25] The text seems to indicate that Jesus' healing here is somehow related to the appearance of the crowd. It is surely safe to say that the miracle was bound up with the wider aspects of Jesus' ministry and that it should not be considered an end in itself.

[26, 27] After Jesus commanded the spirit to come out, the spirit obeyed, although with cries and convulsions. In fact, the boy gave the appearance of being **dead.** Jesus put an end to the doubt of those who were beginning to draw such a conclusion by helping the boy get up off the ground.

[28, 29] The disciples, too, were perplexed about the situation, mainly because they were not able to heal the boy. Jesus, in response to their question as to why they were not able, suggested the need of **prayer** (some ancient authorities add "fasting"). Again, faith on the part of the disciples and the father is one of the most important elements in the story and must be seriously regarded.

It has been observed earlier that references to prayer are uncommon in Mark (contrast Luke) and that when they do appear they may be indications of somewhat severe circumstances (see comments on 1:35). It is signifi-

114

³⁰ **They went on from there and passed through Galilee. And he would not have any one know it; ³¹ for he was teaching his disciples, saying to them, ''The Son of man will be delivered into the hands of men, and they will kill him; and when he is killed, after three days he will rise.'' ³² But they did not understand the saying, and they were afraid to ask him.**

---

cant that the issue comes up in the way that it does here. Jesus seems to be saying to the disciples that their failure to heal the epileptic boy was related to the fact that they had not understood prayer as an expression of complete dependence upon God.

The Second Passion Prediction, 9:30-32 (Matt. 17:22, 23; Luke 9:43b-45)

[30, 31] Jesus is now found to be moving about the countryside in a way that he had not done before. It is possible, of course, to consider even these early movements as a part of Jesus' understanding of himself and an accommodation to the fact of suffering. Jesus may already in his own mind be moving toward Jerusalem and his ultimate sacrifice. The way in which the suffering theme is intertwined with these geographical movements inclines one to favor such a judgment.

Mark specifically mentions that Jesus wanted to move about without anyone knowing it. The reason for this anonymity was that he was teaching his disciples. The purpose seems to be that he wanted time and opportunity to be alone with them that he might speak to them about himself and, of course, that they might more completely understand his purpose (for background read comments on 9:1-13).

In this context Jesus openly spoke of his passion a second time. One has the impression that because modern readers know the end of the story, they find these early passion predicitons more tolerable or acceptable. The disciples apparently went into the events surrounding the crucifixion itself still greatly lacking in their own understanding.

[32] One must stop to examine the purity of the disciples' minds in the original situation. Apparently they were completely baffled by Jesus' passion prediction. As far as they

³³ **And they came to Capernaum; and when he was in the house he asked them, "What were you discussing on the way?"** ³⁴ **But they were silent; for on the way they had discussed with one another who was the greatest.**

---

could see, everything seemed to be going reasonably well. The ministry was developing; men and women were being convicted of their sins and baptized in anticipation of the new kingdom. They might well have asked, "How could any progress be made by means of such disastrous events?"

Mark expresses all this in the simple statement, **They did not understand the saying.** Luke (9:45) adds, almost as an editorial comment, that understanding "was concealed from them," apparently as a deliberate thing. All three synoptic writers mention the difficulty and even fear in the hearts of the disciples because of the nature of this situation. Mark says, **They were afraid to ask.** The disciples simply may not have been willing to expose their ignorance. It may be that they were remembering the scolding that Peter received on an earlier occasion (8:33) when he reacted rather strongly to Jesus' suggestion of suffering and death. The situation might be summarized by observing that although the disciples knew a significant amount about their master, they still have much to learn. One is reminded of the father of the epileptic boy, **"I believe; help my unbelief"** (9:24).

True Greatness, 9:33-37 (Matt. 18:1-5; Luke 9:46-48)

The nature of the situation made apparent in these few verses is in itself quite interesting. Apparently Jesus' question concerning what the disciples had been discussing as they went along the road is based not upon ignorance but upon the fact that he was quite aware. Jesus seems to want to reopen a discussion which he had overheard along the way. In fact, one gets the impression, because of the apparent embarrassment of the disciples, that it was their opinion that Jesus was not aware of their discussion. The story seems to give an insight into the way the group went about. It may be imagined that there were times when Jesus, perhaps preoccupied, went ahead of or behind his disciples.

[33, 34] In any case, Jesus reopened the discussion

³⁵ And he sat down and called the twelve; and he said to them, "If any one would be first, he must be last of all and servant of all." ³⁶ And he took a child, and put him in the midst of them; and taking him in his arms, he said to them, ³⁷ "Whoever receives one such child in my name receives me; and whoever receives me, receives not me but him who sent me."

---

because he had something meaningful to say concerning their lack of understanding. The disciples were embarrassed that they had been discussing the question of their own greatness, that is, the role each was to play in this particular situation.

[35] Jesus **sat down and called them.** He then stated one of his most fundamental and often-repeated principles, **If anyone would be first, he must be last of all and servant of all** (cf. Matt. 20:26, 27; 23:11; Mark 10:43, 44; Luke 22:26; also Matt. 23:12; Luke 14:11; 18:14).

In the kingdom of God there is no greatness in the sense of exalted leadership. Greatness rather comes in the idea of complete service. Paul summarizes the principle, "For what we preach is not ourselves, but Jesus Christ as Lord, with ourselves as your servants for Jesus' sake" (2 Cor. 4:5). In this context, one also recalls Jesus' earlier statement, "If any man would come after me, let him deny himself and take up his cross and follow me. For whoever would save his life will lose it; and whoever loses his life for my sake and the gospel's will save it" (8:34, 35). This principle comes to its most significant point of impact in Christ's own gift of himself. He said, "For the Son of man also came not to be served but to serve, and to give his life as a ransom for many" (10:45).

[36, 37] In the well-known incident of taking a child in his arms, Jesus gave substance to the principle of self-sacrifice. If one **receives** a child in the name of Christ, one somehow receives Christ. In the giving of self in service to man in need, both the giver and the receiver come to a more complete awareness of Christ himself.

Jesus in this connection made one more point. Through the receiving of a child one receives Jesus, and through

³⁸ **John said to him, "Teacher, we saw a man casting out demons in your name,^k and we forbade him, because he was not following us." ³⁹But Jesus said, "Do not forbid him; for no one who does a mighty work in my name will be able soon after to speak evil of me. ⁴⁰For he that is not against us is for us. ⁴¹For truly, I say to you, whoever gives you a cup of water to drink because you bear the name of Christ, will by no means lose his reward.**

^k Other ancient authorities add *who does not follow us*

Jesus one receives the Father. The awareness of God comes through the giving of oneself to those in need. One knows Christ and even God the Father through what he learns in serving his fellow man.

A Lesson in Tolerance, 9:38-41 (Luke 9:49, 50)

This story concerning the strange exorcist apparently concerns an incident in the life of Jesus' followers when he was not with them. The disciples had seen a man casting out demons in Jesus' name (cf. the sons of Sceva, Acts 19:13ff.). The reader is not told what factors caused such an incident but simply that it did happen. Jesus' disciples were disturbed by what they had seen and made some attempt to discourage the man from continuing his practice. Thus the scene is set.

[38-40] Jesus' attitude was considerably more tolerant than that of his disciples. He expresses his attitude very simply in the statement, **No one who does a mighty work in my name will be able soon after to speak evil of me.** Further, Jesus added, **He that is not against us is for us.**

[41] Jesus urged in a very simple and straightforward illustration that genuine discipleship penetrates the most common and mundane things of life. He suggested to his disciples that even those who give his followers a drink —because they are his followers—will receive their reward. Christ may therefore be served in the smallest of ways. Genuine Christianity will express itself in whatever way or ways it finds convenient to any circumstances in which disciples are found.

⁴² "Whoever causes one of these little ones who believe in me to sin,ˡ it would be better for him if a great millstone were hung round his neck and he were thrown into the sea. ⁴³ And if your hand causes you to sin,ˡ cut if off; it is better for you to enter life maimed than with two hands to go to hell,ᵐ to the unquenchable fire.ⁿ ⁴⁵ And if your foot causes you to sin,ˡ cut it off; it is better for you to enter life lame than with two feet to be thrown into hell."ᵐ ⁿ ⁴⁷ And if your eye causes you to sin,ˡ pluck it out; it is better for you to enter the kingdom of God with one eye than with two eyes to be thrown into hell,ᵐ ⁴⁸ where their worm does not die, and the fire is not quenched.

ˡ Greek *stumble*
ᵐ Greek *Gehenna*
ⁿ Verses 44 and 46 (which are identical with verse 48) are omitted by the best ancient authorities

---

Miscellaneous Sayings, 9:42-50 (Matt. 18:6-9; Luke 17:1, 2)

Jesus' teaching is memorable in many ways. It contains a certain amount of humor, satire, vivid imagery, as well as other elements. Teaching that is familiar often escapes the reader because of twentieth-century methods, or indeed because of a lack of understanding of primitive methods. In this case it is necessary to know something about primitive grain grinding.

[42] Millstones of course came in all sizes, from the reasonably small to those that were quite large. If one imagines a millstone weighing hundreds of pounds, Jesus' teaching becomes quite clear. In this way, Jesus urges the importance of caring for his **little ones.** It would be better, Jesus says, to be taken to the bottom of the sea by a millstone, there to die, than to disturb the way of those who did follow him.

[43-48] Jesus further teaches that if one's **hand** is the cause of sin, it should be cut off. Although the inclination is to take Jesus' teaching here in a figurative way, one cannot deny the validity of Jesus' statement, whether figurative or literal. Jesus goes on to make the same point in connection with a **foot** and an **eye.** It should be noted that Jesus frequently employed hyperbole to make his point. Jesus was regularly concerned about the "hearts" of his followers, that is, that

⁴⁹ **For every one will be salted with fire.**ᵒ ⁵⁰ **Salt is good; but if the salt has lost its saltness, how will you season it? Have salt in yourselves, and be at peace with one another.''**

ᵒ Other ancient authorities add *and every sacrifice will be salted with salt*

their inward motivation be pure and in perspective. No amount of the amputation of one's limbs would assure the correct attitude of heart. Verse forty-eight comes from Isaiah 66:24.

[49] It has been indicated that this section consists of a collection of Jesus' sayings. This means, among other things, that content varies significantly. In the case of this saying, the inclusion seems to come because of the association of key words. That is, **fire** is mentioned in the preceding verse and now again here. The subject matter is quite different but the reason for association remains reasonably clear.

Referring to individuals in the kingdom of God, Jesus says, **Everyone will be salted with fire.** There are textual difficulties apparently created because of a certain difficulty in understanding Jesus' meaning. The fact is that salt was a part of Jewish sacrifice (Lev. 2:12; Ezek. 43:24; cf. 8:34-37).

[50] Again by means of the association of key words, Jesus is quoted once more. The verse is divided into three parts: the first two seem to go together, whereas the third may be an independent saying. **Salt** is here considered the necessity of life, perhaps mainly in the sense of a preservative. Jesus' disciples are said to serve as salt to the world. As such they preserve a thing which would otherwise be lost. The warning is given that one should be careful not to endanger or lose his quality of serving in the world as a preservative.

The concluding statement, as has been indicated, should be regarded as an individual saying once again associated because of common words. In this case **salt** may be figuratively equal to ''gospel'' or the ''word'' of God. The disciples then are urged to possess this in themselves and to be able to live at **peace** with one another.

¹ And he left there and went to the region of Judea and beyond the Jordan, and crowds gathered to him again; and again, as his custom was, he taught them.

² And Pharisees came up and in order to test him asked, "Is it lawful for a man to divorce his wife?" ³ He answered them, "What did Moses command you?" ⁴ They said, "Moses allowed a man to write a certificate of divorce, and to put her away." ⁵ But Jesus said to them, "For your hardness of heart he wrote you this commandment.

The Question of Divorce, 10:1-12 (Matt. 19:1-12; cf. Matt. 5:31; Luke 16:18)

[1] Here begins Jesus' movement toward Judea. Mark records only one trip to Jerusalem. There is some indication, particularly in Luke, that there were other such trips. The geographical structure of Mark is in this sense very simple. Jesus' ministry in Galilee and surrounding regions is climaxed by his movement toward Jerusalem and the crucifixion. In this sense there was one consistent purpose, the supreme sacrifice (10:45).

In his travels it was impossible for Jesus to avoid crowds of people. They were compelled to gather around him and he, **as his custom was,** taught them.

[2] It is in this kind of situation that the Pharisees once again make an attempt to trap Jesus. They asked, **Is it lawful for a man to divorce his wife?** Obviously, they were not concerned about the answer to the question but were rather interested in putting pressure on Jesus.

[3-5] Jesus answered by returning a question and at the same time succeeded in throwing the question of the Pharisees back upon the law of Moses. He asked them simply, **What did Moses command you?** They replied that Moses permitted a man to divorce his wife by writing out a statement and giving it to her (Deut. 24:1). Jesus observed that this was because of their **hardness of heart** *(sklēro-kardian).* Jesus seems to be saying that divorce was permitted under the law of Moses primarily because the people were not yet disposed to accept God's original intention. That is, the people were not yet prepared to accept the concept of having only one wife. It is on this basis that

⁶But from the beginning of creation, 'God made them male and female.' ⁷'For this reason a man shall leave his father and mother and be joined to his wife,ᵖ ⁸and the two shall become one flesh.' So they are no longer two but one flesh. ⁹What therefore God has joined together, let not man put asunder.''

¹⁰And in the house the disciples asked him again about this matter. ¹¹And he said to them, "Whoever divorces his wife and marries another, commits adultery against her; ¹² and if she divorces her husband and marries another, she commits adultery.''

ᵖOther ancient authorities omit *and be joined to his wife*

Jesus developed the teaching found in the succeeding verses.

[6-9] In language that is heavily dependent upon the book of Genesis, Jesus reiterated the following principles: (1) from creation there have been, because of God's intention, two sexes; (2) that male is to be joined by female, having grown away from his own parents (the same would of course be true of the female); (3) each pair is to be so united in body and in spirit in such a way that they become **one**; and (4) that this God-created union should not be disturbed by any man.

[10-12] Apparently this teaching appeared to be somewhat hard to the disciples themselves, and they asked Jesus again about it. Matthew records that the disciples went so far as to say that it might be better for them not to marry. Jesus therefore repeated himself and made it quite clear that what he said in the first instance is what he meant. Jesus said, **Whoever divorces his wife and marries another, commits adultery against her.** As is clear in the text, he also stated the converse. Roman law, unlike Jewish, permitted the wife to effect the divorce. Mark records no exceptions and it should be noted that the "except for fornication" clauses are found in Matthew.

In its way this again urges with the greatest clarity that the divine intention was that one man and one woman should find each other in the bonds of marriage and that there they should become a single entity. Any exception to this is less than ideal as far as the divine will is concerned.

122

¹³ **And they were bringing children to him, that he might touch them; and the disciples rebuked them.** ¹⁴ **But when Jesus saw it he was indignant, and said to them, "Let the children come to me, do not hinder them; for to such belongs the kingdom of God.** ¹⁵ **Truly, I say to you, whoever does not receive the kingdom of God like a child shall not enter it."**

The Blessing of the Children, 10:13-16 (Matt. 19:13-15; Luke 18:15-17)

[13] The scene is a touching one; Jesus attracted children (which in itself says something about Jesus). The children wanted to come to him. Jesus' disciples intervened. They apparently felt it their duty to put the children off and, in this way, spare Jesus the nuisance of speaking to them. Not only did Jesus react severly to such an attempt, he used the opportunity to teach a penetrating lesson concerning the kingdom of God.

[14] The attempt on the part of Jesus' disciples to prevent the children coming to Jesus stirred Jesus' anger. He became **indignant** *(ēganaktēsen)*. The verb suggests a strong reaction on Jesus' part, one that indicated he felt his disciples were misunderstanding the basic intent of the kingdom. First he said, **Let the children come to me,** do not hinder them. The force of Jesus' words here put an emphasis upon what he saw as the wrong in the situation. He wanted action and wanted it quickly.

The lesson that Jesus drew out of the incident is first stated **to such belongs the kingdom of God.** In this way Jesus treated the children as symbolic elements of the coming kingdom. The emphasis is not upon the innocent nature of the children but rather on the relation that a child has to his parents. Everything that a child receives at the hand of his parents is a gift. He does not, indeed he cannot earn their attention; he simply receives. The child loves in return.

[15] Jesus did not come to save "innocents"; he came to save sinners. He desired to put sinners into a meaningful relationship with their God. There is nothing that a sinner can do to earn divine favor. God cannot be obligated in this way. Rather, the convicted sinner must simply put him-

¹⁶ And he took them in his arms and blessed them, laying his hands upon them.

¹⁷ And as he was setting out on his journey, a man ran up and knelt before him, and asked him, "Good Teacher, what must I do to inherit eternal life?" ¹⁸ And Jesus said to him, "Why do you call me good? No one is good but God alone.

---

self into a relationship with God in which he is the receiver. It is in this way that he expresses his convictions and his willingness to be obedient.

[16] Jesus apparently made his point. It would appear that his disciples understood what he was saying, inasmuch as they immediately corrected the situation. Jesus separated himself from the lesson concerning the kingdom to take the children in **his arms** and **bless them.**

The Rich Young Ruler, 10:17-22 (Matt. 19:16-22; Luke 18:18-23)

This traditional title is a composite one, "rich" coming from Mark 10:22, "young" from Matthew 19:20, and "ruler" from Luke 18:18. In any case the title is an apt one and the incident, unique in the Gospel, reflects the experience of a severe encounter with Jesus.

[17] This man is characterized as running to Jesus, which perhaps shows his anxiety, and kneeling, which may indicate something of his respect for Jesus. He called Jesus **Good Teacher,** which says nothing about his depth of conviction concerning Jesus' identity. These things, indeed the whole story, make one somewhat concerned to understand the man's motivation. As the text indicates he was a "pious man," and yet there seems to be some doubt. The man's piety is somehow too overt. He seems to need commendation. Indeed, one suspects that he wanted commendation. It may be correct to classify him as an individual religious truth seeker, but in this case the truth seeking somehow seems to have defeated itself. His opening question to Jesus was, **What must I do to inherit eternal life?**

[18] Jesus seems to turn on the man immediately in an attempt to expose his true character. He orginally addresses Jesus as good. Jesus now asks, **Why do you call me good?**

¹⁹ **You know the commandments: 'Do not kill, Do not commit adultery, Do not steal, Do not bear false witness, Do not defraud, Honor your father and mother.' "** ²⁰ **And he said to him, "Teacher, all these I have observed from my youth."** ²¹ **And Jesus looking upon him loved him, and said to him, "You lack one thing; go, sell what you have, and give to the poor, and you will have treasure in heaven; and come, follow me."** ²² **At that saying his countenance fell, and he went away sorrowful; for he had great possessions.**

---

and further cites the fact that goodness is only in God. Jesus is not totally disclaiming greatness in himself or, as some have contended, indicating any awareness of "sin consciousness." Jesus is rather pointing out that the young man's words consist only of conventional flattery.

[19, 20] In this exposure Jesus cites the fifth, sixth, seventh, eighth, and ninth commandments and adds, **Do not defraud.** The young man confidently responds, **All these I have observed from my youth.** One will perhaps always wonder whether the young man was sincere in his naiveté or if he truly had this sort of conviction about the character of his life.

[21, 22] Jesus "saw through" this man; he understood his motivation and knew that if he were to be helped, he would have to be crushed. The text reveals the fact that Jesus could not help **loving** the man. That is to say, Jesus' heart went out to the man in spite of his shortcomings.

In a severe thrust of divine judgment, Jesus opened the way to the man's one most pressing problem, which was his wealth. It should be observed that this man's wealth may have been the financial base for his quest which led him to Jesus in the first place. At least, Jesus makes it clear that the man's wealth had been an obstacle to his own gift of self. In this way Jesus gave instruction that in almost any circumstance would have seemed extremely severe. He suggested to the man that he **sell** his possessions, **give** the money to the poor in order to acquire wealth in **heaven** , and then to **come** with him.

The incident concludes on an extremely sad note. Although Jesus penetrated the heart of the man's problem,

²³ And Jesus looked around and said to his disciples, "How hard it will be for those who have riches to enter the kingdom of God!" ²⁴ And the disciples were amazed at his words. But Jesus said to them again, "Children, how hard it is ' to enter the kingdom of God! ²⁵ It is easier for a camel to go through the eye of a needle than for a rich man to enter the kingdom of God."

' Other ancient authorities add *for those who trust in riches*

---

the man himself could not bear the judgment, at least not at that time. He turned and went away broken-hearted, that is to say, depressed, in low spirits. He had **great possessions** and apparently could not bring himself to part with them. Jesus does not imply in this teaching that all men who desire to follow him must divest themselves of their earthly possessions. Wealth is indeed a problem, as he goes ahead to discuss in the succeeding paragraph, but it does not always separate a man from God.

The Danger of Riches, 10:23-31 (Matt. 19:23-30; Luke 18:24-30)

As one might have expected, following Jesus' encounter with the "rich young ruler" there is a paragraph of teaching concerning riches and the difficulties they may present to that person aspiring to the kingdom of God. As has been observed, Jesus did not teach that it was necessary for everyone to give up wealth in order to be his disciple. Yet, without doubt, wealth does offer many obstacles to people in their attempt to attain genuine righteousness.

[23-25] Jesus begins by observing that it will be extremely difficult, though not impossible, for a rich man to enter the kingdom. He says, **How hard it will be for those who have riches to enter the kingdom of God!** The disciples were apparently somewhat taken back by such a bold, straightforward statement. Apparently because of this difficulty of understanding, Jesus repeated himself. Again being straightforward and emphatic, he supported his statement with an impossible hyperbole. Jesus adds that it would be **easier for a camel** to make its way through **the eye of a needle,** than it would be for a **rich man** to enter **the kingdom of**

²⁶ And they were exceedingly astonished, and said to him,ˢ "Then who can be saved?" ²⁷ Jesus looked at them and said, "With men it is impossible, but not with God; for all things are possible with God." ²⁸ Peter began to say to him, "Lo, we have left everything and followed you." ²⁹ Jesus said, "Truly, I say to you, there is no one who has left house or brothers or sisters or mother or father or children or lands, for my sake and for the gospel, ³⁰ who will not receive a hundredfold now in this time, houses and brothers and sisters and mothers and children and lands, with persecutions, and in the age to come eternal life.

ˢ Other ancient authorities read *to one another*

God. Although tourists to Jerusalem may be shown places in the city wall referred to as "Needle's Eyes," there is no convincing evidence that they were so designated in New Testament times. The statement should be taken simply as Jesus' way of expressing what from a human standpoint was impossible.

[26, 27] The stark bewilderment of the disciples is carried through to completion. Reflecting an exceeding amount of astonishment, the disciples inquire, **Then who can be saved?** They saw clearly the intent of Jesus' figure. It was indeed impossible for a camel to get through the eye of a needle. Jesus was then able to convey the fundamental meaning of his original judgment, **With men it is impossible.** However, he observed, God is not affected by human limitations.

[28-30] Peter almost interrupted to say, **Lo, we have left everything and followed you.** One wonders if Peter is nervously trying to break the intensity of Jesus' message, a thing that might be consistent with his behavior elsewhere. It may be true here also that Peter "did not know what to say" (see 9:6) and yet felt that he simply had to say something. In any case, Peter's statement opened the way for Jesus to supplement what he had already said.

Jesus first emphasized the fact that those who leave either family or possessions will be rewarded **in this time.** That is, there is much to be gained here and now as a result of being a disciple of Jesus. Yet it is not all easy and rewarding. Temporal blessings to the disciple are to be tempered

³¹ But many that are first will be last, and the last first."

³² And they were on the road, going up to Jerusalem, and Jesus was walking ahead of them; and they were amazed, and those who followed were afraid. And taking the twelve again, he began to tell them what was to happen to him,

---

with persecutions. But **in the age to come** the disciple will be rewarded with **eternal life.**

[31] Jesus concluded his remarks by repeating an earlier adage. **Many that are first will be last, and the last first.** Jesus emphasized in these words that the leader of his group—the leader at least by human standards—was not actually the leader but, in fact, the follower. In terms of true Christianity the organization of the group is upside down to what human judgment would have expected (see 9:34ff.; 10:42ff.; etc.).

The Third Passion Prediction, 10:32-34 (Matt. 20:17-19; Luke 18:31-34

In a way this paragraph could be characterized as a straightforward statement of fact. Yet there is in it an ominous overtone, perhaps simply caused by the fact that one knows the outcome. This overtone suggests that things are developing rapidly toward their conclusion.

[32] The disciples were on the way to Jerusalem and Jesus **was walking ahead of them.** He was apparently doing this in such a way that it was observed by those present. Perhaps it was not customary; he may have gone more closely with them most of the time. Whatever the abnormality of the situation, Jesus was ahead of the disciples and leading them in a way that seemingly had not been his custom. There seems to be a certain determination in the way that he carried himself. Some have speculated that Jesus was already, in his mind at least, "in" Jerusalem and going through the difficulties that were to face him there. Surely he was at least mentally preparing himself for the difficult days ahead. And not only was he preparing himself, he was preparing his followers. It is in this kind of situation that Jesus, for the third time, predicted his passion (see 8:31; 9:31).

[33] saying, "Behold, we are going up to Jerusalem; and the Son of man will be delivered to the chief priests and the scribes, and they will condemn him to death, and deliver him to the Gentiles; [34] and they will mock him, and spit upon him, and scourge him, and kill him; and after three days he will rise."

[35] And James and John, the sons of Zebedee, came forward to him, and said to him, "Teacher, we want you to do for us whatever we ask of you." [36] And he said to them, "What do you want me to do for you?" [37] And they said to him, "Grant us to sit, one at your right hand and one at your left, in your glory."

[33, 34] The prediction, which Jesus stated in a very simple way, is made up of the following elements: (1) he was to be **delivered,** (2) **delivered to death,** (3) **mocked,** (4) **spit upon,** (5) **scorned,** and (6) **killed.** The progression found here in Jesus' words is precise, severe, and of course final.

The Request of James and John, 10:35-45 (Matt. 20:20-28; see also Luke 22:24-27)

It is clear that at least some of the disciples felt that Jesus was building some sort of organization. Mark has already recorded one incident in which the disciples questioned among themselves who was the greatest (see 9:33-39). The thinking in the passage at hand is similar. In the building of an organization it is natural that a consideration be given to position, authority, rank, etc. This view would place Jesus at the apex of the organizational structure and his followers in various positions subservient to his.

It is now quite easy to see that Jesus did not have this sort of thing in mind. His "organization" was not to be one in which one individual ranked above the other, but one in which the greatest member was judged to be so because he rendered the greatest service. In this passage Jesus himself finally (see the "great ransom passage," vs. 45) established himself as greatest not because he was the mastermind of the organization, but because he, in his self-sacrifice, gave the greatest gift.

[35-37] Mark records that James and John themselves

³⁸ But Jesus said to them, "You do not know what you are asking. Are you able to drink the cup that I drink, or to be baptized with the baptism with which I am baptized?" ³⁹ And they said to him, "We are able." And Jesus said to them, "The cup that I drink you will drink; and with the baptism with which I am baptized, you will be baptized; ⁴⁰ but to sit at my right hand or at my left is not mine to grant, but it is for those for whom it has been prepared." ⁴¹ And when the ten heard it, they began to be indignant at James and John. ⁴² And Jesus called them to him and said to them, "You know that those who are supposed to rule over the Gentiles lord it over them, and their great men exercise authority over them.

---

came to Jesus with their indirect request. Matthew's account involves the mother of the two boys in the maneuver to share in his **glory**. Jesus responded by asking about their desire. The fact that they came in this way may indicate that they were at least ashamed of themselves. If they were ashamed, it must not have been extreme, for they found it possible to ask Jesus directly to grant them the favored **right-** and **left-hand** positions in his **glory**.

[38-40] Jesus' response, **You do not know what you are asking,** seems to imply that he was at least somewhat surprised that they were even able to make such a brazen request. He may have thought they had achieved a better understanding of his purposes than such a request reflects. He turned on them immediately to ask if they could **drink** his **cup** or be **baptized** with the **baptism** which he was to receive. Both **cup** and **baptism** are metaphorical ways which Jesus used to refer to his passion.

Again, perhaps somewhat brazenly, James and John reply with a strong affirmative, **We are able.** Jesus accepted their statement apparently at face value. One may be reminded at this point that James was ultimately martyred (see Acts 12:2), which indicates that Jesus' judgment was certainly not amiss in the situation. However, Jesus turned their specific request aside, offering no explanation, but saying simply that they were asking him about something over which he had no control.

[41-44] It is not surprising to know that the ten began

⁴³ But it shall not be so among you; but whoever would be great among you must be your servant, ⁴⁴ and whoever would be first among you must be slave of all. ⁴⁵ For the Son of man also came not to be served but to serve, and to give his life as a ransom for many.''

---

to be **indignant** *(aganaktein)* because of the request James and John had made. Jesus took advantage of the situation by teaching a lesson. He cites the Gentiles as those who were famous for developing great organizations in which **authority** was exercised in many different ways. In severe contrast, Jesus said simply, **It shall not be so among you.** He rather suggested that the one who would desire to be great in his following must serve. Indeed, in order to be **first** one must be **slave of all** (see again 9:33ff.).

[45] It is not easy to find strength in weakness or victory in death. And yet these two things represent the basis upon which Christianity was built and the core around which it revolves. Combining the roles of **Son of man** as set out in Daniel (ch. 7) and the Servant of the Lord as it appears in Isaiah (ch. 53), Jesus speaks of himself as one who served and was destined ultimately to give his life. In this, the third declaration concerning his suffering, Jesus says, **The Son of man also came not be served but to serve, and to give his life as a ransom for many.**

The legal term **ransom** *(lutron)* requires some attention. Its appearance in the Septuagint is interesting. It denotes the half-shekel poll tax (Ex. 30:12), the money a man paid to redeem his life because his ox had killed someone (Ex. 21:30), the price of the redemption of the first-born (Num. 18:15), the money used to ransom an enslaved relative (Lev. 25:51f.), and the payment made to recover mortgaged property (Lev. 25:26). Yet it seems impossible to understand the term in this way because of the "to whom" of the ransom with regard to human sin. It seems rather that the concept must be understood positively in terms of the actual working out of the supreme sacrifice of Christ.

Blind Bartimaeus, 10:46-52 (Matt. 20:29-34; Luke 18:35-43)

In this, the second miracle after the confession of Peter, Mark in a unique way shows the role of messiahship as

⁴⁶ **And they came to Jericho; and as he was leaving Jericho with his disciples and a great multitude, Bartimaeus, a blind beggar, the son of Timaeus, was sitting by the roadside.** ⁴⁷ **And when he heard that it was Jesus of Nazareth, he began to cry out and say, ''Jesus, Son of David, have mercy on me!''** ⁴⁸ **And many rebuked him, telling him to be silent; but he cried out all the more, ''Son of David, have mercy on me!''**

it was understood by those who first encountered Jesus. The incident is therefore important.

[46-48] Jesus is still on his way to Jerusalem. He apparently had taken the road down alongside the Jordan River, turning westward near **Jericho** to make the ascent toward Jerusalem. This road was somewhat longer but avoided the difficult hill country. As Jesus was **leaving Jericho,** he encountered a **blind beggar, Bartimaeus.** It should be noted that Bartimaeus is named only in Mark and that Matthew makes a reference at this point to two blind men. The fact that the name is preserved at all may mean that he was personally known in some part of the early church. As there was a multitude with Jesus, Bartimaeus heard their noises as they approached. When he heard that it was Jesus, he immediately began to cry out, **Jesus, Son of David, have mercy on me!** The apparent immediacy and form of his address would seem to indicate that he had some awareness of Jesus and his purposes. The fact that he addressed him as **Son of David**—ordinarily a clear messianic title—must mean that he had some understanding, perhaps incomplete, of Jesus' ultimate purposes. This is not, however, the primary thrust of his interest. From the first, he quite clearly manifested the conviction that he felt Jesus could help him. Bartimaeus nevertheless stirred a reaction among **many** who seemed to have felt that his aggressiveness toward Jesus was out of place. They **rebuked him, telling him to be silent.** But for all their sternness, Bartimaeus seems to have been all the more forward.

These incidents may show something about the nature of Jesus' healing ministry. One feels reasonably secure in the opinion that Jesus did not normally go about healing everyone he encountered who was in physical need. The limited nature of his healing activity seems to be implied

⁴⁹ And Jesus stopped and said, "Call him." And they called the blind man saying to him, "Take heart; rise, he is calling you." ⁵⁰ And throwing off his mantle he sprang up and came to Jesus. ⁵¹ And Jesus said to him, "What do you want me to do for you?" And the blind man said to him, "Master,' let me receive my sight." ⁵² And Jesus said to him, "Go your way; your faith has made you well." And immediately he received his sight and followed him on the way.

' Or *Rabbi*

---

here. In this case, there were **many** who felt Bartimaeus' request to be unseemly or out òf place. This must mean that things were moving in another direction and those who rebuked Bartimaeus would not want to interfere with that movement. Bartimaeus, however, by means of his aggressiveness, overcame their objections.

[49-52] Jesus stopped. He asked that Bartimaeus be called. When Bartimaeus understood that Jesus was calling him, he moved toward Jesus with great concern. Mark at this point is particularly vivid with details which only an observer, presumably Peter (see Introduction) could have made. He records that Bartimaeus, **throwing off his mantle, sprang up** and **came** to Jesus. Jesus asked what he wanted. In his reply, **Master, let me receive my sight,** Bartimaeus expressed a certain faith in Jesus' healing ability.

Jesus told him to go and then, with a somewhat unusual declaration, added, **Your faith has made you well.** Bartimaeus' faith relation to Jesus may have had two dimensions, one in messiahship and the other in "wonder-worker." Bartimaeus' sight was **immediately** restored and he joined the group along with Jesus.

JERUSALEM—JUDEAN MINISTRY, 11:1—12:44

The Triumphal Entry, 11:1-11 (Matt. 21:1-9; Luke 19:28-40; cf. John 12:12-19)

At this point Jesus' life enters its final stages. There is a certain air of finality present. Something akin to the popular concept of Messiah appears for the first time here in the triumphal entry. And although Jesus appears in a way as Messiah, the circumstance is not truly royal but

¹ And when they drew near to Jerusalem, to Bethphage
and Bethany, at the Mount of Olives, he sent two of his disciples, ² and said to them, "Go into the village opposite you,
and immediately as you enter it you will find a colt tied,
on which no one has ever sat; untie it and bring it. ³ If any
one says to you, 'Why are you doing this?' say, 'The Lord
has need of it and will send it back here immediately.' " ⁴ And
they went away, and found a colt tied at the door out in the
open street; and they untied it.

---

rather one of strange debasement. A second element in this
situation has to do with the way in which Jesus acted. There
is a quality within the prophetic activity of the Old Testament
that is often referred to as "prophetic symbolism." This
is manifest in the various ways in which the prophets themselves entered physically into the message they were
attempting to deliver. These sometimes strange activities,
at least for the prophet, were embodiments of the message
he was trying to bring. In this case, Jesus borrowed an
ass upon which to ride into the city. A clue to the meaning
of Jesus' action is found in Zechariah 9:9 where the reader
is told that Messiah would appear "lowly and riding upon
an ass." Zechariah further says that he would "speak
peace unto nations" and have "dominion from sea to
sea." Jesus' action in the paragraph is therefore clearly
messianic — identified with a specific prophecy of the
Old Testament and acted out literally with symbolic
meaning.

[1-3] As the group neared Jerusalem they came to
Bethphage, Bethany, and the **Mount of Olives.** Apparently
with deliberate intent, Jesus sent his disciples into the village
opposite, perhaps Bethphage. They were told that they would
find a **colt** which had never been ridden and that they should
untie it and **bring** it to Jesus. Anticipating the difficulty of
borrowing something that did not belong to them, Jesus
told them that if anyone should ask why they were doing
what they were, that they should say that the **Lord has
need** and that the animal would be returned. Perhaps Jesus
had made some prior arrangement with the owner. Thus,
the stage is set.

[4-6] The disciples went and found the colt just as it

⁵ And those who stood there said to them, "What are you
doing, untying the colt?" ⁶ And they told them what Jesus
had said; and they let them go. ⁷ And they brought the colt
to Jesus, and threw their garments on it; and he sat upon it.
⁸ And many spread their garments on the road, and others
spread leafy branches which they had cut from the fields.
⁹ And those who went before and those who followed cried
out, "Hosanna! Blessed is he who comes in the name of the
Lord! ¹⁰ Blessed is the kingdom of our father David that is
coming! Hosanna in the highest!"

---

had been described. As they were untying it, some of those
standing by did ask them, **What are you doing?** They repeated Jesus' words, which seemed to satisfy them. One
may wonder if the incident should be classed as miraculous
or whether the animal belonged to an acquaintance or
perhaps a friend, and that Jesus had arranged to borrow
it. In either case, the messianic symbolism is being brought
to completion.

[7-10] The animal was brought to Jesus, and after his
friends had put some of their clothing upon it, **he sat upon
it.** The curious "poverty-stricken" yet regal picture that
is given in the passage is genuinely strange. At the same
time, however, the glory of the Messiah appears.

It is certainly possible to examine the situation from
another point of view. There were some who put **their garments on the road,** and yet others who **spread branches,**
and still others **who went before,** and those who **cried out,
Hosanna! Blessed is he who comes in the name of the Lord!**
adding a blessing to the kingdom of David. The salutation
Hosanna is of Hebrew origin and means "save now." The
words come from Psalm 118:25f. and formed the normal
welcome given to people coming to the feast. They are
not in themselves messianic. However, the reference to **our
father David** makes it quite clear that the group here conceived of the total expression in an eschatological sense.
However feeble the faith, however inadequate the insight,
something was realized and something was believed. The
situation — strange, even inadequate — somehow projected
Jesus as Messiah.

135

¹¹ And he entered Jerusalem, and went into the temple; and when he had looked round at everything, as it was already late, he went out to Bethany with the twelve.
¹² On the following day, when they came from Bethany he was hungry. ¹³ And seeing in the distance a fig tree in leaf, he went to see if he could find anything on it. When he came to it, he found nothing but leaves, for it was not the season for figs. ¹⁴ And he said to it, "May no one ever eat fruit from you again." And his disciples heard it.

---

[11] The text of Mark is anti-climatic at this point. Jesus **entered Jerusalem, went into the Temple, looked around,** and **went out to Bethany.** Matthew and Luke include references to Jesus' cleansing the Temple (the same or a similar incident is referred to in John 2:13ff.). Perhaps simply because it was evening and it had been a long day, which included a tiring trip from Jericho, the need for a place to stay became apparent and Jesus turned to physical needs.

The Cursing of the Fig Tree, 11:12-14 (Matt. 21:18f.)

[12-14] The incident described in this brief paragraph and its sequel later in the chapter present a number of difficulties. The problematic nature of the incident may have been sufficient reason for Luke to omit it altogether. On the one hand, it is a miracle of destruction, the only such miracle recorded in the Gospels. Then there are the two statements, **He went to see if he could find anything on it,** and **it was not the season for figs,** each of which makes the other problematic. The difficulties in the passage have caused many commentators to draw severe conclusions. For example, Hunter says, "With our knowledge of Jesus from other sources, we find it frankly incredible that he could have used his power to wilt a fig tree because it would not yield figs two or three months before its mature time of fruitage."

Admittedly there are difficulties. There is indeed the nature of fig trees to be considered. But one might also ask if the incident is out of its proper historical setting. It is possible that Mark has drawn in at this point an incident which actually occurred at another time in the year.

Following Cranfield, one must reckon with the possibility

that the incident could be taken as an "acted parable," in which case Jesus' hunger would have been simply the occasion for the instruction of his disciples. This would imply that Jesus did not expect to find edible figs on the tree, and the statement **it was not the season for figs** should not be challenged, assuming the incident occurred at the time indicated. The fact that Jesus looked for fruit out of season, Cranfield argues, is the very thing that should be expected in parabolic action. That is, one should expect the unexpected as a characteristic feature of symbolic action, as is the case in the prophets of the Old Testament (see Jer. 13:1ff.). He further observes that the earliest extant commentary on Mark by Victor of Antioch views the incident in this way. Victor said that Jesus "used the fig tree to set forth the judgment that was about to fall on Jerusalem." He had accused at least a portion of the Jews of being hypocritical in honoring God with their lips but not with their hearts (see 7:6). They could therefore be likened to a tree with an abundance of leaves but no fruit. In this case, the most apt commentary on these verses is to be found in the incident of the cleansing of the Temple, which is recorded in the succeeding paragraph. This understanding is supported in the fact that the judgment concerning the fig tree is found in the paragraph which follows the one describing the cleansing of the Temple. One then takes Jesus' action in the Temple and his cursing of the fig tree as bearing a specific relation to one another and to some extent as explaining one another (see also comments on vss. 20ff.).

The Cleansing of the Temple, 11:15-19 (Matt. 21:12f.; Luke 19:45-48; cf. John 2:13-17)

Many Christians have viewed Jesus as a soft spoken, quiet person who went about his business in a way that they would call "meek." In this they would see the ideal Christian as that person who gives way to most external forces. Jesus' approach to his own life and work seems for the most part to have been "quiet," but the incident mentioned here when Jesus drove out those who had corrupted the Temple, once and for all dispels the traditional "meek" concept of him. When the occasion demanded it, Jesus could be aggressive, exacting, even forceful. There

137

¹⁵ And they came to Jerusalem. And he entered the temple and began to drive out those who sold and those who bought in the temple, and he overturned the tables of the money-changers and the seats of those who sold pigeons; ¹⁶ and he would not allow any one to carry anything through the temple. ¹⁷ And he taught, and said to them, "Is it not written, 'My house shall be called a house of prayer for all the nations'? But you have made it a den of robbers." ¹⁸ And the chief priests and the scribes heard it and sought a way to destroy him; for they feared him, because all the multitude was astonished at his teaching. ¹⁹ And when evening came they" went out of the city.

" Other ancient authorities read *he*

---

can be no doubt in this incident that he exercised his authority in a dramatic and active way. Any complete picture of Jesus must include the side revealed here.

[15-17] The cleansing of the Temple should be viewed as an act of messianic symbolism. It should be compared in this way with the triumphal entry (vss. 1ff.). The encounter occurred in the outer court or court of the Gentiles which had been converted into a market, apparently for the benefit of the priests. Someone always seems to be available to "work the angles" for their own gain. In order to secure a sale, it was easy to reject any animal brought in by the people for sacrifice. Then, to expedite transactions, there were the money changers.

Jesus found all this quite repulsive. In his statement, **Is it not written, "My house shall be called a house of prayer for all the nations"? But you have made it a den of robbers,** Jesus alludes to Isaiah 56:7 and Jeremiah 7:11. In this way he couched his anger as well as his action in the language of the prophets. Perhaps the most impressive element in the incident is the way Jesus himself appeared standing with and speaking as one of the prophetic tradition.

[18, 19] Such a dramatic incident attracted the attention of the **chief priests** and **scribes** and caused them again to desire Jesus' destruction. (For a similar reference to the Pharisees and the Herodians, see 3:6.) The text goes ahead to say that these men **feared** Jesus and that their fear was linked to the fact that Jesus' teaching was impressive to the multitude. (This factor was mentioned as early as 1:22.)

²⁰ As they passed by in the morning, they saw the fig tree
withered away to its roots. ²¹ And Peter remembered and said
to him. "Master,ᵛ look! The fig tree which you cursed has
withered." ²² And Jesus answered them, "Have faith in God.
²³ Truly, I say to you, whoever says to this mountain, 'Be
taken up and cast into the sea,' and does not doubt in his
heart, but believes that what he says will come to pass, it
will be done for him.

ᵛ Or *Rabbi*

It is not difficult to imagine that Jesus was impressive
in his teaching. Neither is it surprising, at least at times,
that he should be feared. It is, however, striking to notice
that he was feared because of his teaching. The recognized
officials of religion apparently saw in Jesus a serious threat
to their own security.

The brief paragraph concludes with a mention of the
fact that Jesus **went out of the city.** This is an apparent
allusion to his habit of spending the nights in Bethany during
those days immediately before his betrayal and crucifixion.

The Fig Tree and Related Sayings, 11:20-25 (Matt. 21:20-22)

[20-23] The incident of observing the withered tree gave
Jesus an opportunity to speak of the lessons he wanted learned. The fact that they **passed by in the morning** once again
indicates the habit of Jesus and his disciples during these
last days. In their passing, they saw the result of Jesus' curse;
the tree was **withered away to its roots.** Peter observed this
and mentioned it to Jesus. At this point one wonders whether
Peter was surprised or if his tone of voice was simply matter-
of-fact. In any case he felt strongly enough about his observation to comment on it.

Jesus used the opportunity to teach. In a word he says,
Have faith in God. Again it should be noted that faith plays
a significant role in all three miracle stories found after
Peter's confession (see comments on 9:14-29 and 10:46-52).
Such a command on the part of Jesus must be understood
as a kind of summary of the purpose of his whole ministry.
His entire life was devoted to encouraging faith in God on
the part of those who followed him. In this incident Jesus

²⁴ **Therefore I tell you, whatever you ask in prayer, believe that you have received** *ᵃ* **it, and it will be yours.** ²⁵ **And whenever**

ᵃ Other ancient authorities read *are receiving*

---

was so concerned to teach that he couched his principle of faith in extremely strong language. He asserted that if a person does not **doubt** but **believes,** he would be able to **cast mountains into the sea** (cf. 1 Cor. 13:2).

Such a statement has generally been taken figuratively, but it should be observed that Jesus made no hint of this sort. This is not to suggest that Jesus intended the statement to be understood literally, but one should observe the strong, straightforward language having to do with one's relationship of faith to his God. The extreme character of Jesus' language may have no greater purpose than dramatically to call attention to the reality of and need for genuine faith.

If the barren fig tree and the Temple cleansing are to be understood in terms of one another, what specific points may be deduced? Was it the fault of the fig tree that it was not the season? Is it the idea that since fruit-bearing for both the tree and the Temple is past now, that both need to be destroyed, to be replaced with another thing? In this case, the exhortation to have faith is understood as the way above all others to bear fruit in the new kingdom of God. This would make the destruction not simply the result of hypocrisy but a condemnation of shortcomings with a view to a productive future.

[24] The principle concerning faith is followed by two miscellaneous sayings which are at least related in basic content, although they may not properly belong to the incident at hand. Jesus suggested that the person who has faith should pray within that faith and that **whatever** he asks, he will receive. This is not a broad suggestion to extend one's desires fancifully; it is rather a true expression rising out of one's own relationship to God. It cannot therefore be controlled by one's fancy but must always be related to that area of genuine being in relation to the Divine Will that one commonly refers to as faith.

[25] With prayer in the context, another principle is suggested, i.e., that of forgiveness. The willingness to forgive, Jesus says, should be part of every disciple's prayer. And,

140

you stand praying, forgive, if you have anything against any one; so that your Father also who is in heaven may forgive you your trespasses.'"*

²⁷ And they came again to Jerusalem. And as he was walking in the temple, the chief priests and the scribes and the elders came to him, ²⁸ and they said to him, "By what authority are you doing these things, or who gave you this authority to do them?"

*Other ancient authorities add verse 26, *"But if you do not forgive, neither will your Father who is in heaven forgive your trespasses"*

---

as is stated a number of times elsewhere, God's ability to forgive one of his disciples is related to that disciple's willingness to forgive those who have sinned against him. This is simply one way of becoming a servant to all.

The Question of Authority, 11:27-33 (Matt. 21:23-27; Luke 20:1-8)

The very occurrence of this encounter with the official representatives of Jewish religious authority in itself indicates that Jesus had attracted a certain amount of attention. Further, it is probably right to see in this and subsequent encounters certain messianic overtones. One may not always be sure, but the very nature of the situation would seem to favor the appearance of messianic elements.

This encounter is introduced with a question, "By what authority are you doing these things?" This is the first in what appears to be a series of antagonistic confrontations which are all introduced by questions. The others are: (1) "Is it lawful to pay taxes to Caesar or not?" (12:15); (2) "In the resurrection whose wife will she be?" (12:23); and (3) "Which commandment is the first of all?" (12:28). Obviously, this series of incidents is broken by the parable concerning the wicked husbandmen (12:1-12). That the story of the husbandmen, however, is not a genuine interruption is to be seen in the obvious messianic teaching which it, in its parabolic fashion, contains.

[27, 28] The phrase, **they came again to Jerusalem,** once more indicates Jesus' habit of going to and from the city during these last days (see vss. 11, 12, 15, 19, and 20). On this occasion he was confronted by the **chief priests,** the

²⁹ Jesus said to them, "I will ask you a question; answer me, and I will tell you by what authority I do these things. ³⁰ Was the baptism of John from heaven or from men? Answer me." ³¹ And they argued with one another, "If we say, 'From heaven,' he will say, 'Why then did you not believe him?' ³² But shall we say, 'From men'?"—they were afraid of the people, for all held that John was a real prophet. ³³ So they answered Jesus, "We do not know." And Jesus said to them, "Neither will I tell you by what authority I do these things."

---

scribes, and the **elders.** This somewhat unusual delegation is mentioned again later (14:43, 53 and 15:1). The phrasing probably indicates that there were representatives of each of three groups present, which in itself may indicate something of the importance given to the occasion. Their question concerning Jesus' **authority** *(exousia)* for doing **these things** may be based upon his cleansing of the Temple. There may be a messianic overtone in the question itself. If this is true, Jesus was being tempted to betray himself and his intentions openly. His apparent awareness of the real nature of the situation underlines even more the importance of the way in which he handled it.

[**29, 30**] Typically, Jesus answered a question with a question. He promised to answer their question if they would answer his. He asked concerning the **authority** behind John the Baptist; indeed, was John **from heaven** or **from men?** Again one may see messianic overtones. John had in his way pointed toward the appearance of the Messiah, and if they accepted John as being **from heaven,** they would be obligated seriously to consider Jesus.

[**31-33**] Such a question caused them to turn to one another, for they immediately saw the dilemma in which Jesus had put them. On the one hand, if they accepted John, they would automatically raise some question about their own lack of response to him; on the other hand, if they openly concluded that John was only human, they might suffer at the hands of the people, for **all** thought that John was a **real prophet.** Because they would have found themselves in difficulty by selecting either of the alternatives suggested by Jesus, they declared their ignorance. And

142

¹ **And he began to speak to them in parables. "A man planted a vineyard, and set a hedge around it, and dug a pit for the wine press, and built a tower, and let it out to tenants, and went into another country. ² When the time came, he sent a servant to the tenants, to get from them some of the fruit of the vineyard.**

---

because they would not answer Jesus' question, he was not obligated to answer theirs.

In this way the real intention of this group of antagonists was turned aside. Jesus knew that there was no point in answering their question, for they were not really seeking answers. Their obvious purpose was to ensnare Jesus and he cleverly escaped their trap. Yet his counter question was a veiled claim to heavenly **authority.**

The Wicked Husbandmen, 12:1-12 (Matt. 21:33-46; Luke 20:9-19)

Although this paragraph is commonly referred to as a parable, it is in fact more allegorical in character than most of Jesus' parables. Jesus himself occasionally interpreted his parables along allegorical lines (see e.g., 4:12-20). Most modern scholars subscribe to the principle that Jesus told most of his parables to point up one basic lesson or concept. No allegorical significance, however, belongs to many of the details, and Jesus could have used some features in the story to make a pointed application to his opponents.

Messianic elements once again appear in the wider context. It is difficult to resist the idea that Jesus was thinking of himself when he mentioned the beloved son (vs. 6). One must always remember, though, that elements of this type are always clearer looking back than they were at the time of their origin.

[1, 2] Jesus set the situation quickly in a very straightforward fashion, borrowing details from Isaiah 5:1f. There was a man who set out to establish a **vineyard** — planting it, protecting it, and arranging for the necessary equipment to conduct its operation. Having made his investment and turning it over to what he thought to be responsible people, he went into **another country.** At the time when he would

³ And they took him and beat him, and sent him away empty-handed. ⁴ Again he sent to them another servant, and they wounded him in the head, and treated him shamefully. ⁵ And he sent another, and him they killed; and so with many others, some they beat and some they killed. ⁶ He had still one other, a beloved son; finally he sent him to them, saying, 'They will respect my son.' ⁷ But those tenants said to one another, 'This is the heir; come, let us kill him, and the inheritance will be ours.' ⁸ And they took him and killed him, and cast him out of the vineyard. ⁹ What will the owner of the vineyard do? He will come and destroy the tenants, and give the vineyard to others. ¹⁰ Have you not read this scripture:

---

have expected some return from his original investment, he sent a **servant** to collect it.

[3-5] The brevity of Jesus' first description is underscored by the fact that he spent more time discussing the various servants sent to collect the owner's portion of the profits than he did describing the original outlay. In simple fashion, and yet in starkly grim terms, Jesus described how the investor sent three servants, one after another, to collect the rent. These men suffered all sorts of injuries, maltreatment, and abuse at the hands of the tenants. Thus the stage is set for the last and most significant effort on the part of the owner.

[6] In clear messianic terms, Jesus described the fact that the owner of the vineyard had one **beloved son** and, arguing with himself that the tenants would **respect** his son, he sent him.

[7, 8] When the tenants observed that the **heir** was coming to collect the rent, their immediate reaction was to suggest to one another that, if they killed him, the **inheritance** would belong to them. So they did and **cast him out of the vineyard.**

The fact that Jesus refers to the owner's **beloved son** is not the only messianic element in the passage. The concept of an underserved as well as unjustified death points at Jesus himself in greater detail than has been the case previously. Again, this may be more apparent looking back.

[9-11] At this point Jesus asked, **What will the owner**

'The very stone which the builders rejected
has become the head of the corner;
¹¹this was the Lord's doing,
and it is marvelous in our eyes'?''
¹² And they tried to arrest him, but feared the multitude,
for they perceived that he had told the parable against them;
so they left him and went away.
¹³ And they sent to him some of the Pharisees and some
of the Herodians, to entrap him in his talk.

---

of the vineyard do? Replying immediately to his own rhetorical question, Jesus suggested that the owner would appear, destroy the tenants, and **give the vineyard to others.** Once more the backward view makes it possible to see a direct application to the Jewish nation. Their rejection was at least part of the reason that God's gift was given to others (see e.g., Acts 13:46). This is developed further by Jesus' quotation of Psalm 118:22f., where the **stone rejected** by the **builders** comes finally to be **the head of the corner.** A link is perhaps supplied with the use of this same Psalm in 11:10.

[12] The directness of the parable was understood by those who desired to **arrest him** (see 11:27), a fact which in itself gives some confirmation to the idea that the parable was told with certain messianic intent in mind. They did not act because they were afraid of the crowd and not being able to accomplish their desire, **they left him and went away.**

The Question about Taxes, 12:13-17 (Matt. 22:15-22; Luke 20:20-26)

The second in this series of confrontations concerns the question of paying taxes to the Roman government. Again, according to Mark, the Pharisees and the Herodians (see 3:6) were responsible for the question. It was the intention of Jesus' opponents in this incident to trap him on the horns of a dilemma. In response, Jesus established the one basic principle to be found in the Gospels concerning the relation of his disciples to the state.

[13] The purpose of the opposition to Jesus at this point must have been obvious. All the synoptics agree that these men came for the expressed purpose of creating difficulty

¹⁴ And they came and said to him, "Teacher, we know that you are true, and care for no man; for you do not regard the position of men, but truly teach the way of God. Is it lawful to pay taxes to Caesar, or not? ¹⁵ Should we pay them, or should we not?" But knowing their hypocrisy, he said to them, "Why put me to the test? Bring me a coin,ˣ and let me look at it."

ˣ Greek *a denarius*

---

for Jesus and discrediting him. They wanted, the text says, **to entrap him in his talk.**

[14] However, before putting the specific question that they had designed, they approached Jesus with what can only appear as conventional and therefore distasteful flattery. They complimented Jesus for being **true** *(aletheia)*, that is, real, genuine, authentic. Beyond this, Jesus' opponents made two statements which concerned the fact that he was not false with any man. First, they said that Jesus did not **care** for any man in the sense of showing partiality. That is, that he did not allow the **position** of any individual to blur the message which he wanted to convey. This is borne out in the second statement, **you do not regard the position of men.** Rather, the opposite was true; they saw that Jesus truly taught the way of God. On the basis of this extremely accurate but unfairly motivated assessment, they put their question, **Is it lawful to pay taxes to Caesar, or not?**

[15] The text reveals that Jesus was actually aware of their **hypocrisy** and therefore set about to find a means of showing the insincerity in the question. The tension in the incident is supplied in the implication that Jesus' opponents had the trap securely set. If he answered negatively, they could accuse him of being an insurrectionist. If he answered in the affirmative, he would make himself appear to be a weak Messiah. Jesus asked for a **denarius.** He did not ask to see the coin because he was unaware of what was inscribed upon it but rather as a means of showing the fallacy of the questioner's position. The very fact that they could produce such a coin means, of course, that they were committed to the use of the currency, and for them the question he had in mind was already answered.

¹⁶ And they brought one. And he said to them, "Whose likeness and inscription is this?" They said to him, "Caesar's." ¹⁷ Jesus said to them, "Render to Caesar the things that are Caesar's, and to God the things that are God's. And they were amazed at him.

[16, 17] After receiving the coin Jesus asked them, **Whose likeness and inscription is this?** They of course replied, **Caesar's**, at this time Tiberius. That the questioners used Roman currency showed their own ackowledgment of an obligation to Rome. Then Jesus stated the principle that they should give both **to God** and **to Caesar** the things that rightfully belong to each.

This unique statement contains the essence of Jesus' teaching on the subject: there is no necessary conflict between one's allegiance to his political unit and his devotion to God. It is obvious, of course, that in spite of Jesus' statement there have been many conflicts in the history of man between what one owes to God and what one owes to the state. According to Jesus, this conflict should not be considered inevitable.

If one would get a complete picture of the teaching of the New Testament with regard to the state, it would be necessary to examine Romans 13:1-7; 1 Timothy 2:1-6; 1 Peter 2:13-17, and Revelation 13, as well as those passages dealing with the present rule of Christ. There have been and will be governments which, either by their very nature or by their means of operation, create a conflict between the dual nature of the Christian's allegiance. The New Testament quite clearly teaches that if a choice of any sort is required, one's devotion to God is primary and must therefore be judged the more important.

The Question concerning the Resurrection, 12:18-27 (Matt. 22:23-33; Luke 20:27-40)

It is commonly understood that the doctrine of the resurrection, although latent within the structure of Judaism, gained a certain popularity in the century or so prior to the appearance of Jesus. The Sadducees distinguished themselves in that they opposed this development. They felt that

¹⁸ **And Sadducees came to him, who say that there is no resurrection; and they asked him a question, saying,** ¹⁹ **"Teacher, Moses wrote for us that if a man's brother dies and leaves a wife, but leaves no child, the man**ʸ **must take the wife, and raise up children for his brother.** ²⁰ **There were seven brothers; the first took a wife, and when he died left no children;** ²¹ **and the second took her, and died, leaving no children; and the third likewise;** ²² **and the seven left no children. Last of all the woman also died.** ²³ **In the resurrection whose wife will she be? For the seven had her as wife."**

ʸ Greek *his brother*

God's judgments would all be effected in this life. This conviction, and their opposition to what was probably the more widely held view, gave them the necessary basis upon which to question Jesus. Their logic must be complimented, at least from their point of view. Jesus quickly pointed out their inadequacies, but as they originally conceived it, the question was quite valid.

[18, 19] The text begins by stating the fact that the Sadducees appeared before Jesus. They prepared the ground for their question by reviewing the law of Moses, which had said that a man was responsible for raising up children to his brother's name if that brother died childless. In fact, the law said that he was to "perform the duty of a husband's brother" (Deut. 25:5).

[20-23] Reviewing this aspect of the Mosaic law, the Sadducees described what surely must have been a hypothetical situation, although it would not have been completely out of the realm of possibility. There were, they said, **seven brothers,** and the wife of the first had borne no children when her husband died. In accordance with the law, the second of the brothers **took her** and the same thing happened again. The picture is drawn in the most extreme terms; according to the Sadducees, all six brothers took the responsibility of raising children to their first brother's name. They were very careful to stress that it was only after the death of all seven brothers that the woman herself died. On this ground they put the question, **In the resurrection whose wife will she be?**

Given the presuppositions mentioned earlier, the ques-

²⁴ Jesus said to them, "Is not this why you are wrong, that you know neither the scriptures nor the power of God? ²⁵ For when they rise from the dead, they neither marry nor are given in marriage, but are like angels in heaven. ²⁶ And as for the dead being raised, have you not read in the book of Moses, in the passage about the bush, how God said to him, 'I am the God of Abraham, and the God of Isaac, and the God of Jacob'? ²⁷ He is not God of the dead, but of the living; you are quite wrong."

---

tion of the Sadducees is unanswerable. One can almost see them pausing, quite happy with themselves, awaiting Jesus' attempt to answer a question which showed the idea of resurrection to be a practical absurdity.

[24, 25] The accusation of Jesus is immediate and extremely direct. He charged that they were wrong on two points: they understood neither **the scriptures** nor the **power** *(dunamis)* **of God.** Jesus then proceeded to deal with the second point first. The Sadducees had completely overlooked the fact that the spiritual world of the hereafter was to be completely different from the natural world within which their question had been framed. There is no marriage after the resurrection but rather an angelic sort of existence. The spiritual world of the angels would not even admit the possibility of physical union of the type implied in the Sadducees' question.

[26, 27] Then Jesus argued that the resurrection concerned living individuals who, by their very character, do not properly belong to the dead. He observed that the Old Testament often implied that Abraham, Isaac, and Jacob were not dead but alive (see Ex. 3:6; cf. Matt. 22:31f.). The conception is that men who belong to God in faith live on, even though they may be no longer in existence physically. Resurrection is then viewed as a divine act through which these men will achieve the fullness of life originally intended in creation and lost by means of sin and resultant physical death. On the basis of his observation about these great Old Testament characters, Jesus then urged, **He is not God of the dead, but of the living.** And then with a final statement almost as startling as the opening

²⁸ And one of the scribes came up and heard them disputing with one another, and seeing that he answered them well, asked him, "Which commandment is the first of all?" ²⁹ Jesus answered, "The first is, 'Hear, O Israel: The Lord our God, the Lord is one; ³⁰ and you shall love the Lord your God with all your heart, and with all your soul, and with all your mind, and with all your strength.' ³¹ The second is this, 'You shall love your neighbor as yourself.' There is no other commandment greater than these."

---

remark, Jesus concluded, **You are quite wrong.** The stage is thus set for the final question.

The Question of the First Commandment, 12:28-34 (Matt. 22:34-40; cf. Luke 10:25ff.)

[28] The question concerning the first commandment (see comments on 11:27ff.) is the last in a series of four and seems to represent a different attitude on the part of the questioner. This time the question comes from **one of the scribes,** and there does not seem to be in the text the same explicit desire to trap Jesus that is present in the preceding incidents. One wonders if the scribe may have overheard at least a part of the previous exchange and had perhaps admired Jesus' ability to respond. This question may therefore be quite serious in intent, the scribe genuinely desiring to know how Jesus would respond to a question disputed among the rabbis. He asks, **Which commandment is the first of all?**

[29-31] Jesus quickly responded to the question with a biblical answer that would not only be undeniable in its origin but would encompass "the whole duty of man." **First,** quoting Deuteronomy (6:4f.), Jesus unequivocally states that **love** of **God** is the element most desired in one's religious life. Without any hesitation he adds a **second,** quoting Leviticus (19:18), that one should **love** his **neighbor** as himself.

On reflection, one observes that the first commandment in fact includes the second. One could not love God without loving his fellow man (1 John 4:20), although some have tried it. On the other hand, it may well be that Jesus adds the second here because human experience so often finds its way to the first by means of the second. That is, by loving man one comes to love God.

³² And the scribe said to him, "You are right, Teacher; you have truly said that he is one, and there is no other but he; ³³ and to love him with all the heart, and with all the understanding, and with all the strength, and to love one's neighbor as oneself, is much more than all whole burnt offerings and sacrifices." ³⁴ And when Jesus saw that he answered wisely, he said to him, "You are not far from the kingdom of God." And after that no one dared to ask him any question.

³⁵ And as Jesus taught in the temple, he said, "How can the scribes say that the Christ is the son of David?

[32-34] Somewhat surprisingly, the scribe in question had sufficient courage to discuss with Jesus the answer that had been given. In his way the scribe extended an elaborate compliment to Jesus, particularly with regard to his ability to teach. What he said apparently made some favorable impression on Jesus. The scribe's answer reflects the attitude of 1 Samuel 15:22 and Hosea 6:6. The text remarks that Jesus saw that he **answered wisely.** Returning a compliment for a compliment, Jesus said, **You are not far from the kingdom of God.** The paragraph closes with the statement, **And after that no one dared to ask him any question.** The statement should probably not be taken to mean that in this incident Jesus once for all stopped those who opposed him, but rather that Jesus' ability to answer his questioners put an end to their desire to question him. Jesus was frustrating their objectives by turning their opposition to his own advantage.

David's Son or Lord? 12:35-37 (Matt. 22:41-46; Luke 20:41-44)

It is difficult to imagine what particular set of circumstances preceded and developed into the incident described here. Conflict has been suggested, and may very well have been a part of this background. If this is true, then the question Jesus raised may have originally been a diversion. However, because of the arresting content of the question, the Gospels show no extensive interest in the original circumstances.

[35-37] Jesus asked, **How** — that is, in what sense — **is the Christ** ("the Messiah") to be thought of as the descen-

> [36] David himself, inspired by ᶻ the Holy Spirit, declared,
> 'The Lord said to my Lord,
> Sit at my right hand,
> till I put thy enemies under thy feet.'
> [37] David himself calls him Lord; so how is he his son?" And
> the great throng heard him gladly.

ᶻ Or *himself, in*

dant of **David?** Jesus observed that certain difficulties arose when one recalled that David spoke of this person as his **Lord.** Jesus quoted from Psalm 110, which in his day was attributed to David. The question, in other words, is: In what sense can the Messiah be both the son and Lord of David? The fact that **the great throng heard him gladly** may indicate a sort of hero response, perhaps because Jesus was so capable of putting precise as well as incisive questions to the supposed authorities of his day.

Once again it is obvious that Jesus is not asking for information. Neither is he concerned to secure a current popular exegesis of Psalm 110. In addition to the possibility that the question may have originally served as a diversion, Jesus is concerned to get interested people to think out the precise meaning of messianic sonship. He understood himself to be **Lord** *(kurios)*, and as such, a much more important figure in the divine scheme than **David.** He also knew that his followers, if they were to get the complete benefit of his person, must come to understand this. A response in faith was necessary.

The phrase translated, **inspired by the Holy Spirit,** is in the original literally, "in the Holy Spirit." It was the Holy Spirit talking, and David was in fact only the divine instrument in the process (see also Acts 1:16, 28:25; 2 Tim. 3:16; 2 Peter 1:21).

This text makes it clear that for Jesus the title **son of David,** correct as far as it went, was inadequate. If his followers desired a more complete understanding, it would be necessary for them to go beyond this terminology. The obvious ramifications make this particular text of no small importance in observing Jesus' own understanding of messiahship.

³⁸**And in his teaching he said, "Beware of the scribes, who like to go about in long robes, and to have salutations in the market places** ³⁹**and the best seats in the synagogues and the places of honor at feasts,** ⁴⁰**who devour widows' houses and for a pretense make long prayers. They will receive the greater condemnation."**

Beware of the Scribes, 12:38-40 (Luke 20:45-47; cf. Matt. 23; Luke 11:37—12:1)

Jesus was certainly not opposed to complimenting a perceptive scribe (see vss. 28-34), although he is more remembered for his awareness of their false motives. Indeed, in this context Jesus has already made some serious implications about the teaching being done by the scribes (vss. 35-37). Now he turns to certain of their practices. It may be that Jesus' teaching here was orginally conceived as an explicit application of the lesson found in verses 1-12, that is, that the leaders and teachers of the nation have proved unfaithful husbandmen and fully merited the condemnation which is in store for them.

[38, 39] **Robes** is a reference to a common outer garment known as a *tallith*. There is evidence that the scribes wore a particularly large version of this garment and were therefore known for the way in which they appeared. These **robes** attracted attention and were accompanied by certain **salutations,** as well as by a desire for the **best seats in the synagogue** and the **place of honor at feasts.** There can be no doubt that there were many quiet, industrious scribes who understood their task and did it. However, this text recognizes some who could not separate themselves from the glory of their situation and, in fact, went to certain lengths to increase the public attention given to them. Such a practice completely misses the point of public service, a principle which needs to be kept in mind by all public servants, especially those that purport to be servants of God.

[40] Jesus is, of course, concerned about the hypocrisy of this minority. They appeared to be one thing in their public lives, while within themselves they were something quite different. Any man who manufactures **long prayers** for his own purposes and turns from them — or perhaps

⁴¹ **And he sat down opposite the treasury, and watched the multitude putting money into the treasury. Many rich people put in large sums.** ⁴² **And a poor widow came, and put in two copper coins, which make a penny.** ⁴³ **And he called his disciples to him, and said to them, "Truly, I say to you, this poor widow has put in more than all those who are contributing to the treasury.**

---

uses them — to take advantage of **widows** merits any condemnation or exposure he may receive.

The Widow's Mites, 12:41-44 (Luke 21:1-4)

Associations with the Temple in the wider context may account for the presence of this story at this particular point, although it should not be forgotten that the thought of "widow" is in the author's mind (see vs. 40). This incident may therefore be included here on the "catchword" principle noted earlier (see 1:2). The story stands in contrast to those scribes who "devour widow's houses."

No supernatural awareness by Jesus is necessary to account for this episode. It is quite conceivable that Jesus first sensed the circumstances of the situation, perhaps by the expression on the woman's face.

[41] The precise meaning of the word **treasury** (*gazophulakios*) is in some doubt. The word was originally used to refer to a certain room in the Temple which was reserved for the storage of valuables (see 1 Macc. 14:49; 2 Macc. 3:6). In the context at hand it seems to refer to some receptacle for the offerings of worshipers. According to the Mishnah, there were thirteen trumpet-shaped containers placed around the wall of the court of the Women for this purpose. The reference may therefore be to these. However, it is possible on the basis of this text to suggest a receptacle within the treasury—thought of as a room—but having some sort of opening on the outside through which offerings might be made.

[42] The widow put in **two copper coins** (*lepta duo*), **which make a penny.** The *lepton* was the smallest Greek coin. Mark explains that two were equivalent to the Roman *quadrans,* worth one sixty-fourth of a *denarius* (vs. 15).

[43, 44] Unlike the story of the woman with the alabaster

154

⁴⁴**For they all contributed out of their abundance; but she out of her poverty has put in everything she had, her whole living."**

---

jar (14:3-9), Jesus' disciples made no comment about the incident. It may be that they did not even see it, as the text says that Jesus **called his disciples to him** that he might enlarge upon the obvious but subtle magnitude of the gift. This point is made emphatic with the two phrases, **everything she had . . . her whole living.**

It is more difficult for a rich man to enter heaven simply because of the virtual impossibility of his making any real sacrifice and thereby coming to know the devotion of that kind of discipleship (see 10:17-31). Large gifts out of abundance simply cannot be compared with the total gift of one's poverty. Cranfield comments, "The gifts of the rich, though large, were easy gifts; the widow's gift, though tiny, meant a real surrender of herself to God and trust in him, and therefore an *honouring* of God *as God,* as the one to whom we belong wholly and who is able to care for us."

THE MARKAN APOCALYPSE, 13:1-37

Introduction to Mark 13

Authenticity. Contrary to some, it is the conviction of this commentary that chapter 13 represents sayings which in fact came from Jesus but which have a dimension backward from his time (through the use of earlier materials) and belong to a context subsequent to his time. One should, on the one hand, not be surprised to find language reminiscent of earlier works (such as Daniel) and therefore in some sense dependent upon them. On the other hand, the actual writing of the chapter was done by Mark and therefore incorporates a tension and concern for at least some of the things that were a part of his historical situation (the imminent destruction of Jerusalem). This leads to both of the succeeding assumptions.

Unity. Mark saw this particular part of his work—whatever may be noted of its diverse elements—as one unit. Evidence of this is abundant. The reference to "this" *(tauta,* vs. 4a) refers back to verse two, whereas the mention of "these things" *(tauta,* vs. 4b) reaches across to verses

29 and 30. "Take heed" *(blepete,* vs. 5) may also include a reference to verse 2. This statement is repeated in verses 9 and 33. Further references to time are scattered through the chapter: "the end is not yet" (vs. 7); "this is but the beginning of the sufferings" (vs. 8); "the gospel must first be preached" (vs. 10); "then . . . flee" (vs. 14); "if anyone says" (vs. 21); "after that tribulation" (vs. 24); "then they will see" (vs. 26); "and then he will send" (vs. 27). In themselves alone, these statements surely imply Mark's view of the whole as one unit.

Consistency. It is also the view of this commentary that the unity of chapter 13, just referred to, is a part of Mark's overall consistent purpose. It is reasonable to conclude that Mark set out to write with a specific grand purpose in mind for the entire Gospel and that that purpose includes chapter 13. When it is recalled that Mark 13 was written *after* the events recorded in chapters 14-16, and that at the time of writing the primitive church was corporately facing difficulties — especially in Jerusalem (that is, if the traditional dating of A.D. 66-70 is correct) — not unlike those that Jesus personally faced earlier, one finds chapter 13 to offer hope of the most profound kind, particularly to those who were feeling the pinch of the Roman advance. In this light, the hortatory words (esp. vss. 33-36) take on particularly relevant and urgent meaning. This contemporary theological content of the chapter must not be overlooked.

Mark's situation. Perhaps the most important element in a consideration of this particular aspect of the chapter is to be found in Jesus' transitional phrase, " . . . this is but the beginning *(archē)* of the suffering" (vs. 8). If one allows that the specific times mentioned prior to that statement (i.e., messianic pretenders and wars) had in fact already been experienced by the time of writing, then it follows that Mark understood Jesus' statement as applicable to his own moment in time as a part — if only the "beginning" — of "the end." Though many things were to happen "in this generation" (vs. 30), neither Mark nor Jesus (see vs. 32) knew exactly when "that day" would come (more about this apparent contradiction later). The important thing here is to see the tension current to Mark's own time as a part of the total picture.

This line of argument may be pursued further. It may be necessary to understand that all of the specifics mentioned through verse 13 were experienced by Mark or representatively known to have happened prior to the time of writing. Repetitions might of course occur later. This view puts considerable emphasis upon the future quality implicit in the phrase, "when you see" *(hotan . . . idete,* vs. 14). An implication with this quality is not found earlier. It is at least true to say that "when" *(hotan)* is not attached to an unrepeatable specific prior to this point. This would explain that it is Mark — not Jesus — who said, "let the reader understand" (vs. 14). The punctuation in the RSV seems to indicate that its translators understood the phrase in this way. This understanding seems necessary in any case since what is presented here to the reader as a part of Mark's Gospel had its origin as a private discourse with a selected group of disciples (see vs. 3). This would mean that Mark, as mentioned earlier, understood certain contemporary events as "the beginning of the sufferings," understood as a part of "the end," however obscure the time factor. The imminent destruction of the Temple, now taken literally (see comments on vs. 2), was then understood as the next event in the sequence (vss. 14-23). But that was not all; there was more to come (vss. 24ff.). Mark's readers must be careful to interpret the signs correctly (vss. 28ff.), but ultimately — again, whatever the time factor — "the end" in the narrow and final sense will come (vss. 32ff.). Such an understanding clearly underlines the undeniable viability of the ever imminent return of the Lord, which must be understood as basic to the Christian system. Among other things, this is to say that, if anything, "the end" must have seemed nearer to that inhabitant of Jerusalem in the late 60s of the first century who could look out over the city wall and see the Roman army than it does to modern man who has some vague awareness of the nuclear capability of contemporary war machines but has not seen it for himself. The essential message, therefore, is "Watch!"

Apocalyptic. Although apocalyptic represents a literary form that was fairly well confined historically, the severe elements that cause its production are to some extent present in every age, and there has therefore been a continuing

interest in the message of these works. Perhaps the one
which best exemplifies this observation is John's Revelation.
Even yet, feelings from the "overtones" of such a document
sometimes substitute for the firmer convictions of more
"normal" exegesis.

Apocalyptic as a literary genre was produced from about
175 B.C. with the persecution of Antiochus Epiphanes
until near A.D. 135 or the failure of the Bar Kochba re-
volt. Reaction to political turmoil and oppression was
an essential element in its generation. What was a valid way
of speaking about contemporary events often became the
esoteric production of the intellectually elite, a group as
elusive as one's own estimate of his intellectual prowess.

Generally speaking, apocalyptic literature was controlled
by a deep dualistic conviction. This has been defined as
the "cosmic and eschatological belief in two opposing cosmic
powers, God and Satan (or his equivalent); and in two distinct ages — the present, temporal, and irretrievably evil
age under Satan, who now oppresses the righteous but whose
power God will soon act to overthrow; and the future,
perfect and eternal age under God's own rule, when the
righteous will be blessed forever." This deep theological
concern for deliverance, basic to apocalyptic literature,
may be clearly seen in Mark thirteen. There can be no serious
doubt that it is correct to think of this chapter as a part of
this broad literary phenomenon.

It is tempting to urge that the chapter is more eschatological then apocalyptic. In this regard, one cannot, of course,
deny that at least half of the area of concern (see vs. 4)
lies right here. The point, however, is that even these eschatological elements are treated in an apocalyptic manner.
And, although by its very nature precise interpretation is
impossible — perhaps even undesirable — the end result
of the combination is an emphasis upon the theological importance of the basic message embedded in this literary
form. This must not be overlooked. God will triumph!

Notes on Mark 13 (Matt. 24:1-36; Luke 21:1-36)

In chapters 11 and 12 an awareness of impending doom
is developed. This, of course, is only after a certain awareness of the nature of Jesus' messiahship is secured. In the

158

¹ And as he came out of the temple, one of his disciples said to him, "Look, Teacher, what wonderful stones and what wonderful buildings!" ² And Jesus said to him, "Do you see these great buildings? There will not be left here one stone upon another, that will not be thrown down."

³ And as he sat on the Mount of Olives opposite the temple, Peter and James and John and Andrew asked him privately, ⁴ "Tell us, when will this be, and what will be the sign when these things are all to be accomplished?" ⁵ And Jesus began to say to them, "Take heed that no one leads you astray.

---

cursing of the fig tree (11:12-14, 20-22) and the cleansing of the Temple (11:15-19) the existing Jerusalem order is doomed. The story of the wicked tenants (12:1-12) and the attempts to trap Jesus (12:13-34) point directly to his purposes. Now Jesus announces the destruction of Jerusalem. With chapter 13 Jesus' ministry is complete; the crowd, mentioned a number of times in the two preceding chapters (11:8, 18, 32; 12:12, 37, 41), disappears to reappear only in chapter 15 to request the release of Barabbas.

[1, 2] (Additional comments on vs. 2 may be found in the chapter introduction. See also comments on 8:34.)

Jesus' mention of the destruction of the Temple was one of his more popularly known sayings (see Mark 14:58; 15:29; John 2:19; Acts 6:14). The saying caused considerable confusion among his hearers and provoked later reflection on its spiritual meaning in reference to his body (see John 2:21, 22). There were apparently a number of "difficult" sayings of Jesus that had this sort of retroactive significance. The fact that the "destruction of the Temple" is regularly referred to figuratively makes this reference here in chapter 13 all the more interesting, because here it is obvious that Jesus is not speaking about his body but rather very literally about the Temple itself. It is in this way that the severity of the situation is vividly called to the reader's attention. He cannot but pay attention to this radically different set of circumstances (cf. however the repetition of the figurative concept at 14:58).

[3-8] (See also chapter introduction on vss. 3, 4, 5, 7, and 8.)

The observations of Jesus' disciples were made **as he**

⁶ Many will come in my name, saying 'I am he!' and they
will lead many astray. ⁷ And when you hear of wars and
rumors of wars, do not be alarmed; this must take place,
but the end is not yet. ⁸ For nation will rise against nation,
and kingdom against kingdom; there will be earthquakes in
various places, there will be famines; this is but the beginning
of the birth-pangs.

⁹ "But take heed to yourselves; for they will deliver you
up to councils; and you will be beaten in synagogues; and
you will stand before governors and kings for my sake, to
bear testimony before them. ¹⁰ And the gospel must first be
preached to all nations. ¹¹ And when they bring you to trial
and deliver you up, do not be anxious beforehand what you
are to say; but say whatever is given you in that hour, for
it is not you who speak, but the Holy Spirit. ¹² And brother
will deliver up brother to death, and the father his child,
and children will rise against parents and have them put to
death; ¹³ and you will be hated by all for my name's sake.
But he who endures to the end will be saved.

---

came out of the temple, and Jesus' reply began **as he sat
on the Mount of Olives.** For the significance of the change
between an answer begun to the disciples (vs. 5) and the
address to the reader (vs. 14), see the Introduction.

The blending of the destruction of the Temple and the
end of the world must confirm the view that it is here understood that the two things—however far they may ultimately
be separated in time—were two parts of the same thing.

Contemporary messianic pretenders (see also comments
on vss. 21ff., cf. John 5:43) and wars are to be understood
as **the beginning** of the sufferings but not **the end.** The very
nature of the statement **the end is not yet** is such that it
seems designed to counter what was thought to be a misunderstanding. In any case, one of the basic messages embedded in these verses is, whatever you do, do not overlook the
signs.

[9-13] (See also the introductory comments on vss. 9,
10, and 13.) The specifics mentioned may describe the com-
munities of the Diaspora. However, **governors, kings,** etc.,
were also a part of the Palestinian scene of the day. This
would argue for a completely localized setting.

¹⁴ "But when you see the desolating sacrilege set up where it ought not to be (let the reader understand), then let those who are in Judea flee to the mountains; ¹⁵let him who is on the housetop not go down, nor enter his house, to take anything away; ¹⁶and let him who is in the field not turn back to take his mantle. ¹⁷And alas for those who are with child and for those who give suck in those days! ¹⁸Pray that it may not happen in winter. ¹⁹For in those days there will be such tribulation as has not been from the beginning of the creation which God created until now, and never will be. ²⁰And if the Lord had not shortened the days, no human being would be saved; but for the sake of the elect, whom he chose, he shortened the days.

The thoughts in verses 9-11 are related if not intertwined. At least it should be agreed that verses 9 and 11 speak essentially of the same thing. An interim is clearly predicted; the **gospel must be preached.** One is reminded of Romans 11:25 where time is to be given "until the full number of the Gentiles come in." Here, however, the suggested interim makes up an argument that "the end is not yet."

The guidance of the Holy Spirit for those who found themselves called upon to witness under difficult circumstances is a well-known part of messianic promise (see also Matt. 10:19, 20; Luke 12:11, 12; John 14:26; 15:26; 16:7-11).

[14-20] (See also the introductory comments on vss. 14 and 21.)

Attention should again (see p. 157) be drawn to the fact that Mark now addresses his **reader** (cf. vs. 3).

A question arises here immediately concerning the **desolating sacrilege.** At this point it is tempting to over interpret by means of the allegorical method. In this case, however, one feels at least slightly more secure than is the case most of the time. The term **desolating sacrilege** *(bdelugma tēs erēmōseōs)* must surely be related to Daniel (9:27; 11:31; 12:11). It has been associated with the altar of Zeus which Antiochus caused to be erected in the Temple area in 168 B.C. (cf. 1 Macc. 1:54). Later, in about A.D. 40, one P. Petronius was ordered to erect the emperor Caligula's image in the Temple. There was a delay and Caligula's murder

²¹ And then if anyone says to you, 'Look, here is the Christ!' or 'Look, there he is!' do not believe it. ²² False Christs and false prophets will arise and show signs and wonders, to lead astray, if possible, the elect. ²³ But take heed; I have told you all things beforehand.

²⁴ "But in those days, after that tribulation, the sun will be darkened, and the moon will not give its light, ²⁵ and the stars will be falling from heaven, and the powers in the heavens will be shaken. ²⁶ And then they will see the Son of man coming in clouds with great power and glory. ²⁷ And then he will send out the angels, and gather his elect from the four winds, from the ends of the earth to the ends of heaven.

---

in A.D. 41 prevented the execution of the plan. Again, however, a similar thought was in the air.

Consistent with this background, Mark, in typical apocalyptic fashion, seems to see the Roman army fulfilling the role as agent in the destruction of the Temple. There can be no doubt that Jesus' earlier prediction which was understood to apply to the "temple of his body" is now replaced (cf., however, 14:58 where the earlier thought is again repeated). Here the literal destruction of the Jerusalem Temple marks the prelude to **the end.** It would appear that Mark saw the sacrilege as a fulfillment of the destruction of the Temple.

The predicted destruction is to be so immediate and sudden that there will be no time for second-thought preparation (vss. 15, 16; on vs. 17, cf. Luke 23:29). Recognizing the inevitability of the disaster, one can only pray that the timing of the event will at least slightly lessen the personal hardship (vss. 18-20). It is understood that God has himself responded to this situation with appropriate action.

[21-23] Messianic pretenders are regularly seen as a part of the signs (see also vs. 6; on the deception theme, see Rev. 13:13ff.). The foretelling of this phenomenon is designed to render their appearance patently false (see John 16:1, 4).

[24-27] (See also chapter introduction on vss. 24, 26, and 27.) The desolation predicted here is clearly separated from that discussed earlier in the chapter by the phrase

²⁸ "From the fig tree learn its lesson: as soon as its branch becomes tender and puts forth its leaves, you know that summer is near. ²⁹ So also, when you see these things taking place, you know that he is near, at the very gates. ³⁰ Truly, I say to you, this generation will not pass away before all these things take place. ³¹ Heaven and earth will pass away, but my words will not pass away.

³² "But of that day or that hour no one knows, not even the angels in heaven, nor the Son, but only the Father. ³³ Take heed, watch; ᵃ for you do not know when the time will come. ³⁴ It is like a man going on a journey, when he leaves home and puts his servants in charge, each with his work, and commands the doorkeeper to be on the watch. ³⁵ Watch therefore—for you do not know when the master of the house will come, in the evening, or at midnight, or at cockcrow, or in the morning—³⁶ lest he come suddenly and find you asleep. ³⁷ And what I say to you I say to all: Watch."

ᵃ Other ancient authorities add *and pray*

---

after that tribulation. The cosmic order will be disturbed, the climax being the appearance of the **Son of man.** This is to be followed by the gathering of the **elect** (see 1 Thess. 4:16, 17).

[28-31] (Also see chapter introduction on vss. 29 and 30.) The faithful should be able to read the "signs of the times" and thereby know (at least by faith) that literally earth-shattering events are in the offing. The **he** of verse 29 may be understood as a backward reference to the "desolating sacrilege" of verse 14 and not a reference to the Son of man (vs. 26). This would make sense of the reference to **this generation.** It has been clearly established that a great deal of what Mark saw as a part of the immediate future was to be understood as but "the beginning of the sufferings" (concerning the immenence of the event see James 5:8f.).

[32-37] (See also chapter introduction on vss. 32-36.) Of the exact time of the final cosmic disaster nothing is known. The implication seems to be that it was especially designed this way. One should give his energies to radical preparation. **Watch!** (cf. Matt. 25:5; Acts 20:31; Rev. 3:20).

163

¹ It was now two days before the Passover and the feast of Unleavened Bread. And the chief priests and the scribes were seeking how to arrest him by stealth, and kill him; ² for they said, "Not during the feast, lest there be a tumult of the people."

THE PASSION NARRATIVE, 14:1—16:8

The Conspiracy against Jesus, 14:1, 2 (Matt. 26:1-5; Luke 22:1, 2)

It is a well-known fact that the early Christians proclaimed the resurrection (see the sermons in Acts) but apparently felt that they had to explain the cross. It may well be that many of the technical problems which are present in the various Gospel accounts at this point (e.g., whether or not the Sanhedrin could function as a court—see comments on 14:63, 64) are there because the early church was not attempting to construct an ordered account of the events themselves, but was rather trying to answer questions like; How could Jesus' death be good news? How could Messiah be from Nazareth? Or, on what grounds could such a person be condemned? Indeed, it is quite likely that both the length and content of the passion narrative were severely affected by questions such as these.

[1, 2] A foreboding presence is embedded in this passage due to the commitment which had been made to kill Jesus. The time is obviously growing short. The imminence of Jesus' death is clearly in the air. There is common agreement among the leaders of the people to dispose of Jesus. It must, they thought, be done discreetly; one can never anticipate the reaction of the people. Jerusalem was always subject to the whims of the people, and control of the Jerusalem mob was always a distinct advantage. An example of the inability, even of the Romans, to be in complete control of the city at a later date is exemplified by the fact that 470 soldiers were gathered to escort Paul out of the city at night when the reaction of a mob was feared (Acts 23:23). Though the Jewish officials in this present passage are resolved to wait until after the Passover, the willingness of Judas to involve himself in the situation caused them to reconsider. **Chief priests** designated the high priest,

³ And while he was at Bethany in the house of Simon the leper, as he sat at table, a woman came with an alabaster flask of ointment of pure nard, very costly, and she broke the flask and poured it over his head. ⁴ But there were some who said to themselves indignantly, "Why was the ointment thus wasted? ⁵ For this ointment might have been sold for more than three hundred denarii,ᵇ and given to the poor." And they reproached her. ⁶ But Jesus said, "Let her alone; why do you trouble her? She has done a beautiful thing to me. ⁷ For you always have the poor with you, and whenever you will, you can do good to them; but you will not always have me. ⁸ She has done what she could; she has anointed my body beforehand for burying.

ᵇ The denarius was a day's wage for a laborer

captain of the Temple, directors of the daily and weekly courses, the treasurer — in other words the permanent Temple overseers. (On high priest see also 11:18; 14:43, 53ff.; 15:3.)

The Anointing at Bethany, 14:3-9 (Matt. 26:6-13; cf. John 12:1-8)

[3] This episode almost appears as an interruption in the sequence of events. To say the least, it is an unusual story to be included in an account of a man's death. The unusual nature of the incident seems to imply that it was included by the writer for a significant and definite reason. It may be doubtful that the woman thought of herself as anointing the Messiah. It is nonetheless clear that Mark wanted his readers to see the messianic significance of the woman's action. If she sensed simply the imminence of Jesus' death, her action—as the passage indicates (vs. 8)—may be understood as premature in anticipation of Jesus' death. In this way the foreboding established at the beginning of the chapter is carried another step forward.

[4-8] Christ's disciples reacted negatively to the woman's extravagent **waste** of the ointment. It was, they said, worth the average working man's wage for approximately a year and might have been a great help to the poor. Yet Jesus defended the woman's act and rebuked

⁹ And truly, I say to you, wherever the gospel is preached
in the whole world, what she has done will be told in memory
of her."

¹⁰ Then Judas Iscariot, who was one of the twelve, went
to the chief priests in order to betray him to them.

---

the disciples, saying that she had done **what she could, a
beautiful thing.**

[9] This woman's act should perhaps be regarded as a
classic sermon in silence, for Jesus commented, **what she
has done will be told in memory of her.** The woman said
nothing, but in her action had preached one of the most
meaningful and articulate of sermons. The incident then
becomes one of the most dramatic examples of the inter-
penetration of event and gospel, for in effectively drawing
out the meaning of the incident one must know something
of the "good news" about Jesus. In this unique story a
tremendous gift in terms of love and sacrifice is expressed.
Jesus defended the woman's extravagance because he recognized the depth of what she had done.

The Betrayal, 14:10, 11 (Matt. 26:14-16; Luke 22:3-6)

[10] The willingness of **Judas** to cooperate in the removal of Jesus caused the leaders of the people to alter their
earlier decision not to make any move during the feast. The
earlier fear of the Jewish leaders turned into jubilation
as it became apparent that rather than oppose Jesus'
removal, the people would in fact support it. The appearance
of Judas must have contributed substantially to the morale
of those who opposed Jesus.

One wonders whether Judas' act of betrayal was in
pointing Jesus out or simply indicating his whereabouts.
If Judas' task was to point out which man was Jesus, the
chief priests feared the possibility of arresting the wrong
man. Perhaps the appearance of Jesus was known by the
leaders but not by the Temple soldiers making the arrest. It
would seem, however, that Judas' betrayal had more to do
with Jesus' whereabouts. There had to be general awareness
of who Jesus was to give credence to the initial fear of the
multitude if Jesus should be taken in public. The primary

¹¹ And when they heard it they were glad, and promised to give him money. And he sought an opportunity to betray him.

¹² And on the first day of Unleavened Bread, when they sacrificed the passover lamb, his disciples said to him, "Where will you have us go and prepare for you to eat the passover?"

---

concern must have been the when and where of convenience and not any fundamental question of identity.

How did Judas persuade himself that it was the right thing to do to **betray** Jesus? One must assume that his action was not sinister. Did Judas, as some have suggested, think to set in motion a chain of events that would somehow ultimately make Jesus the recognized Messiah (whatever content Judas himself may have given to that term)? It would appear that Judas was as surprised as anyone that his action led to Jesus' death. What is the meaning of this? The possibility must be granted that Judas sincerely thought that he was contributing to the rightful working out of the divine scheme. Apparently Judas felt that Jesus would be victorious (in Judas' definition of terms) in any confrontation with the established authority and would therefore not be killed. Yet, Jesus was killed, and because Judas' plan went amiss, he killed himself. At the very minimum, Judas must have found it difficult—as did the others, including Peter—to accept Jesus' own understanding of messiahship.

[11] It is extremely difficult to think that the money had much to do with Judas' action, although it is possible. John does speak of Judas as being greedy (John 12:3-8). He records the fact that Judas was the treasurer for the apostles, that he had taken money for his own purposes, and that it was Judas who raised the question about the woman wasting the ointment (see preceding section). One must therefore leave open the possiblity that there was a link between the three hundred denarii and the thirty pieces of silver.

Preparation for the Passover, 14:12-16 (Matt. 26:17-19; Luke 22:7-13)

[12] The Passover is upon them. It is interesting to note

¹³ And he sent two of his disciples, and said to them, "Go into the city, and a man carrying a jar of water will meet you; follow him, ¹⁴ and wherever he enters, say to the householder, 'The Teacher says, Where is my guest room, where I am to eat the passover with my disciples?' ¹⁵ And he will show you a large upper room furnished and ready; there prepare for us." ¹⁶ And the disciples set out and went to the city, and found it as he had told them; and they prepared the passover.

¹⁷ And when it was evening he came with the twelve. ¹⁸ And as they were at table eating, Jesus said, "Truly, I say to you, one of you will betray me, one who is eating with me." ¹⁹ They began to be sorrowful, and to say to him one after another, "Is it I?" ²⁰ He said to them, "It is one of the twelve, one who is dipping bread into the dish with me.

---

that Jesus' disciples assumed that Jesus intended to observe the feast and asked simply **where** he wanted them to make the necessary preparations. This and other incidents show that Jesus was a law-abiding Jew.

[13, 14] Jesus sent two disciples (cf. 11:1-6) into Jerusalem to follow **a man carrying a jar of water,** surely an unusual occurrence to say the least, as women normally performed this task. There is the possibility that this was a pre-arranged sign that Jesus had made to avoid some difficulty. More likely it was the exercise of his divine insight.

[15, 16] There has been a certain interest in the **upper room.** In Acts 1, after the ascension, the fact is mentioned that the visiting apostles had found lodging in an upper room. Could there be any link with Mary's house (Acts 12), an established center for the early church in Jerusalem, the certain young man (14:51, 52), and the upper room of the supper and the apostles' lodging? It is only a possibility of course, but it is one that would draw Mark into the events concerning Jesus at a very early stage and thereby lay the base upon which he later became a leader of some importance (see comment on 14:51, 52).

The Prediction of the Betrayal, 14:17-21 (Matt. 26:20-25; Luke 22:14, 21-23)

[17-20] Another development occurs in the fatal chain

²¹ For the Son of man goes as it is written of him, but woe to that man by whom the Son of man is betrayed! It would have been better for that man if he had not been born.''

²² And as they were eating, he took bread, and blessed, and broke it, and gave it to them, and said, ''Take; this is my body.''

---

of events. The divine plan is in operation. Christ and **the twelve** are described as being **at table**, a verb which suggests reclining on cushions at a low table. What should otherwise have been a happy occasion was turned just the opposite with Jesus' prediction of his betrayal. **They began to be sorrowful.** Part of the point here has to do with the sharing of food, a thing taken seriously in the culture of the time. The fact that table fellowship was taken to indicate friendship and good will may serve as an indication of Judas' attitude toward what he was doing. It is not likely that Judas could have thought of himself as an enemy of Christ and observe this act of friendship. It is more likely that Judas had convinced himself that he was doing the right thing in betraying Christ. In this way Judas in good faith could eat guiltlessly with Christ.

The prediction made the disciples exceedingly curious. They were baffled, perhaps even dumbfounded, that anyone, particularly one so close, could do such a thing. They each reacted only to the possibility of himself doing the deed, not the likelihood of anyone else in the group. Such an attitude can only be commended. The custom of **dipping into the dish** was common. The main bowl was left in the center of the table and was shared by dipping morsels of bread into it.

[21] Jesus' warning concerns the inevitability of the Son of man going **as it is written.** Yet, at the same time there is a strong **woe** to the betrayer. Naturally, anyone involved in what was to result in the death of Jesus would have had a great burden to bear after the fact. The warning was probably not intended as a final condemnation but as a statement of fact. There were two men in the group who were to fall short of what Jesus himself would have desired—Judas and Peter—and their two reactions dramatically show two vastly different ways of dealing with guilt.

²³ And he took a cup, and when he had given thanks he gave it to them, and they all drank of it. ²⁴ And he said to them, "This is my blood of the ᶜ covenant, which is poured out for many.

ᶜ Other ancient authorities insert *new*

The Institution of the Supper, 14:22-25 (Matt. 26:26-29; Luke 25:15-20)

[22] The institution that Jesus effected was very much a part of the Passover celebration, as it was accomplished **as they were eating.** The background is important. It should be remembered that unleavened bread was a part of that first Passover meal the night before the children of Israel departed from Egypt. And bread and wine were the elements Melchizedek shared with Abraham after the latter had defeated the coalition of kings that had set themselves against him (Gen. 14). Christ's similarities with the priest Melchizedek are well known (see Heb.). The word **blessed** refers to the Jewish form of thanksgiving, "Blessed be thou, O Lord God, who gives bread. . . ." Thus there is considerable evidence that the Lord's Supper should be thought of as having been established upon earlier elements of the Jewish tradition.

[23, 24] By sharing in the **bread** and the **cup,** the **body** and **blood** according to Jesus, the partaker is made to share in the incarnation itself. The Supper brings the participant into contact with the fleshly presence of Jesus in the participant's world. Thus the Supper is spiritual food, but it is also more than that. It brings about a forced confrontation with the incarnation. In these elements, in the institution made by Christ himself, one is brought to deal with Jesus' absolute identification with man. Without the incarnation there could have been no Supper. Jesus' incarnation established a new **covenant** (cf. Ex. 24:8) not limited to one race. The reason or end of the incarnation was the saving death (Heb. 2:14ff.). Covenants were associated with blood (Ex. 24:6-8; Heb. 9:11-14). The Supper, then, is an act in which the participant becomes physically involved in the revelation of the concrete reality of God incarnate.

²⁵ Truly, I say to you, I shall not drink again of the fruit
of the vine until the day when I drink it new in the kingdom of God."

²⁶ And when they had sung a hymn, they went out to the
Mount of Olives. ²⁷ And Jesus said to them, "You will all
fall away; for it is written, 'I will strike the shepherd, and
the sheep will be scattered.' ²⁸ But after I am raised up, I
will go before you to Galilee." ²⁹ Peter said to him, "Even
though they all fall away, I will not." ³⁰ And Jesus said to
him, "Truly, I say to you, this very night, before the cock
crows twice, you will deny me three times." ³¹ But he said
vehemently, "If I must die with you, I will not deny you."
And they all said the same.

---

[25] The Supper is observed as a remembrance of Jesus,
his life, work, and death. It is not merely a memorial of
his death, for Jesus himself was not satisfied that it should
be simply a looking back. He instituted it with a forward or
future aspect also, as he spoke of a **day** when he would
drink it new in the kingdom of God (Luke 13:29; 14:15; Isa.
25:6).

*Peter's Denial Prophesied, 14:26-31 (Matt. 26:30-35; Luke
22:39)*

[26-28] The hymn seems to close the Passover observance. They walked across to the **Mount of Olives** and later,
specifically, Gethsemane. Once again Jesus was attempting
to lead his followers to a deeper understanding of what was
happening, not only predicting that the **shepherd** would be
struck (see Zech. 13:7; cf. John 16:32) but that reunion
would take place in **Galilee.**

[29-31] Peter, at this point, is brought once again into
sharp focus. Mindful of an earlier incident (8:31ff.), Peter
is sure of himself in a way that needed correction.

It makes interesting speculation to wonder just how much
Peter actually knew at this point. He knew some things, surely a significant amount more than he did earlier (again, see
8:31ff.), but he was still ignorant, certainly, of many other
things.

The prediction concerning denial in Peter's case is very

171

³² **And they went to a place which was called Gethsemane; and he said to his disciples, "Sit here, while I pray." ³³ And he took with him Peter and James and John, and began to be greatly distressed and troubled. ³⁴ And he said to them, "My soul is very sorrowful, even to death; remain here, and watch."ᵈ ³⁵ And going a little farther, he fell on the ground and prayed that, it it were possible, the hour might pass from him.**

ᵈ Or *keep awake*

---

specific, so specific that its fulfillment was devastating. Part of the point, of course, is to put Peter under a great amount of pressure in order to prepare him at least partially for greater things. Therefore, the situation was developed by Jesus in such a way to put Peter through a greater strain than any of the others. This focus on Peter is carried right to the end of the paragraph with his almost violent denial of the prediction and his promise to be loyal even unto death. In all probability, Peter did not yet recognize that it was Jesus' lot to die. The emphasis in the statement was most probably upon the **if**, thus indicating Peter's relative ignorance of Jesus' immediate fate.

The Gethsemane Incident, 14:32-42 (Matt. 26:36-46; Luke 22:40-46)

[32] The incident recorded here clearly depicts the two vastly different levels on which various members of the group at this point were thinking. Jesus was under the severe stress of his impending fate, while his disciples, content for the most part to be with their master, were largely oblivious to what was happening around them. Jesus' need for prayer must be taken seriously. It shows the humanness of the situation, as well as his dependence upon the Father.

[33, 34] Once again Jesus shows his preference for the "inner core" of his disciples, Peter, James, and John, and, in the process (vs. 37), shows his great regard for Peter. The depth of Jesus' agony is more apparent here than perhaps anywhere else in the Gospel. The two phrases, **greatly distressed and troubled** and **soul . . . very sorrowful, even unto death,** vividly demonstrate this. These are phrases more to be apprehended emotionally than intellectually.

[35, 36] Jesus, **on the ground,** prayed that **if. . . possible,**

172

³⁶ And he said, "Abba, Father, all things are possible to thee; remove this cup from me; yet not what I will, but what thou wilt." ³⁷ And he came and found them sleeping, and he said to Peter, "Simon, are you asleep? Could you not watch one hour? ³⁸ Watch *d* and pray that you may not enter into temptation; the spirit indeed is willing but the flesh is weak." ³⁹ And again he went away and prayed, saying the same words. ⁴⁰ And again he came and found them sleeping, for their eyes were very heavy; and they did not know what to answer him. ⁴¹ And he came the third time, and said to them, "Are you still sleeping and taking your rest? It is enough; the hour has come; the Son of man is betrayed into the hands of sinners. ⁴² Rise, let us be going; see, my betrayer is at hand."

d Or *keep awake*

---

the hour might pass from him. This prayer may in itself say something about Jesus' own understanding of the events before him. The possibility of an alternative must have been a real thing in Jesus' mind (cf. Heb. 5:7f.). This would seem to be confirmed by his statement, **all things are possible to thee.** One of the things that clearly emerges from the situation is Jesus' determination to face what previously he had been reluctant to face (see vss. 41f.). Yet it must be observed that throughout his agony his **will** was subject to the **Father.** For the combination of the Aramaic and Greek words for **Father** see Romans 8:15; Galatians 4:6.

[37-40] Here is seen the weakness of the **flesh** both in Jesus and the disciples. It was not that the disciples were unconcerned; they simply did not know, and this was complicated by the fact that they were tired. Jesus, in so clearly showing his need, is showing the depth of his own humanity. Thus one sees side by side the greatest urgency and the inability to be concerned.

[41, 42] The paragraph concludes with what may be Jesus' own coming to understand that his immediate future will in fact contain the event he most severely dreaded. That is, it must and will happen in this way, and his **hour** had, in fact, **come.** There is a finality in Jesus' words as they prepare to leave that has not heretofore been detected.

⁴³ And immediately, while he was speaking, Judas came, one of the twelve, and with him a crowd with swords and clubs, from the chief priests and the scribes and the elders. ⁴⁴ Now the betrayer had given them a sign, saying, "The one I shall kiss is the man; seize him and lead him away under guard." ⁴⁵ And when he came, he went up to him at once, and said, "Master!"ᶜ And he kissed him. ⁴⁶ And they laid hands on him and seized him. ⁴⁷ But one of those who stood by drew his sword, and struck the slave of the high priest and cut off his ear. ⁴⁸ And Jesus said to them, "Have you come out as against a robber, with swords and clubs to capture me? ⁴⁹ Day after day I was with you in the temple teaching, and you did not seize me. But let the scriptures be fulfilled."

ᶜ Or Rabbi

The Betrayal, 14:43-50 (Matt. 26:47-56; Luke 22:47-53)

[43-46] The words **Judas came** are some of the most ominous in the Gospel. Here again a certain strangeness is encountered (see comments on 14:10f.). The language, **the one I kiss is the man,** seems to imply that those who intended to take Jesus were uncertain of his identity. While this is possible, it is somewhat difficult to accept. Perhaps the darkness made such an act necessary.

[47-49] It is not compatible with the thinking of most Christians that there should have been any violence initiated by Jesus' disciples. It would even seem strange to most that Peter (see John 18:10) had a sword with him, although Luke contains a curious and often overlooked paragraph in this connection (Luke 22:35-38). To say the very least, there is a tension suggested in the fact that Jesus deplored their coming after him, weapons in hand, and the violent reaction of his disciple. The healing of Malchus (John 18:10) would seem to show Jesus' opposition to any use of force, especially in this situation. In Matthew 26:52, 53 Jesus is quite explicit in this regard. His reference here to his **teaching** and his statement, **let the scriptures be fulfilled,** show rather his acceptance of what must be (cf. vs. 21). There is no explicit mention of any Old Testament passage, but Isaiah 53 seems to be behind Mark's consideration of Jesus' death (cf. 9:12; 10:45; 14:42). In any case, the emphasis

[50] **And they all forsook him, and fled.**

[51] **And a young man followed him, with nothing but a linen cloth about his body; and they seized him,** [52] **but he left the linen cloth and ran away naked.**

[53] **And they led Jesus to the high priest; and all the chief priests and the elders and the scribes were assembled.** [54] **And Peter had followed him at a distance, right into the courtyard of the high priest; and he was sitting with the guards, and warming himself at the fire.**

---

on the necessity of the fulfillment of scripture is significant (vs. 49; cf. Luke 24:26, 44ff.; and esp. Acts 2:23ff.). The point is not that Christ's death was predicted but that it was absolutely necessary. It was a part of God's saving plan.

[50] In marked contrast to their sleeping in the garden, when the disciples sensed the nature of the situation, **they forsook him and fled.** How vastly things changed in so short a period of time!

A Certain Young Man, 14:51, 52

[51, 52] The **young man's** identity is not disclosed. Perhaps he was sleeping in the house where Jesus ate the last supper and rose hastily from bed out of curiosity about what was happening so as to follow Jesus to Gethsemane. If the house were that of Mary, the mother of John Mark (where the disciples met at a later date, Acts 12:12; see also the "upper room" of Acts 1:13), it is possible that the **young man** was the evangelist himself. This thesis has some confirmation in the fact that these verses have no parallel in any of the other Gospels.

Jesus' Trial and Peter's Denial, 14:53-72 (Matt. 26:57-75; Luke 22:54-71)

Before Jesus could be crucified, it was necessary for the Jews to convince the Romans that it was the thing to do. While there were several phases involved in these events —structured somewhat differently by the various Gospel writers—Mark mentions only the trial before the high priest and the council, the confirmation of the council after daybreak, and the resultant handing over to Pilate (15:1) for official Roman trial and condemnation.

[53, 54] First, Jesus was taken to the **high priest,**

175

⁵⁵ Now the chief priests and the whole council sought testimony against Jesus to put him to death; but they found none. ⁵⁶ For many bore false witness against him, and their witness did not agree. ⁵⁷ And some stood up and bore false witness against him, saying, ⁵⁸ "We heard him say, 'I will destroy this temple that is made with hands, and in three days I will build another, not made with hands.' " ⁵⁹ Yet not even so did their testimony agree.

Caiaphas. A significant amount of anticipation had encouraged preparation: **the chief priests, elders,** and **scribes** constituted the Sanhedrin. That they were waiting for Jesus' appearance shows the tension in the situation. The reminder that **Peter followed** must be seen as an intrusion into the narrative. It appears intentionally as a preparation for his denial later in the chapter (vss. 66ff.).

[55-59] The first order of business was to see what evidence they might have against Jesus so that they might construct a case to present to the Roman authorities. They found their case to be remarkably impoverished of clear evidence and accusation. Some of the evidence was manufactured for the occasion, and consequently there was disagreement. The primary charge concerned the destruction and rebuilding of the Temple. Jesus had made such a prediction (13:2), although such language was more often associated with the "temple of his body" (John 2:21). Jesus' prediction was, of course, known (15:29; cf. Acts 6:14). The phrase **made with hands** (vs. 58) is sometimes found as polemical language against idols (Acts 7:48; 17:24). The concept of building the Temple was in the tradition connected with David (2 Sam. 7:11b). It would have been natural to associate this with the son of David, *the* anointed. It was easy therefore, in such a context, for Caiaphas to speak about Jesus as the Christ.

It is not necessary to dwell upon the fact that the trial was a legal fiasco, quite contrary to what one gathers from later sources about Jewish legal proceedings (but see comments on vs. 64). This is the strongest sort of evidence concerning the way in which the circumstances contributed to what happened.

⁶⁰ And the high priest stood up in the midst, and asked Jesus, "Have you no answer to make? What is it that these men testify against you?" ⁶¹ But he was silent and made no answer. Again the high priest asked him, "Are you the Christ, the Son of the Blessed?" ⁶² And Jesus said, "I am; and you will see the Son of man seated at the right hand of Power, and coming with the clouds of heaven." ⁶³ And the high priest tore his garments, and said, "Why do we still need witnesses? ⁶⁴ You have heard his blasphemy. What is your decision?" And they all condemned him as deserving death.

[60-62] The interchange between Jesus and the high priest is one of the most important in the Gospel. Jesus' restraint is remarkable; the anxiety of Gethsemane is no longer part of the situation. The question, **Are you the Christ, the Son of the Blessed?** is the most direct and appropriate put to Jesus anywhere in the Gospel. Precisely conceived from a Jewish point of view (e.g., **the Blessed** One as a substitute for the name of God), it has embedded in it a clear concept of messiahship. It is the one completely correct identity question directed at Jesus in the Gospel (see Introduction). Consequently, Jesus' answer is also the most direct found in the Gospel, **I am.** . . . The immediate switch back to the third person **Son of man** statement—with all its implications (see Introduction)—is not without significance. That is, Jesus' answer is also clearly messianic and is an effort to give content to what was meant by messiahship. The conceptual world of Daniel 7 is apparent both in thought and implication.

[63, 64] It is clear that the high priest understood the implications both of his own question and particularly of Jesus' reply, because he labeled it **blasphemy**, that is, making oneself equal with God. In suggesting himself to be God—at least equal with God—Jesus posed a threat to Jewish monotheism as it had been popularly conceived. One can imagine that it must have struck the average Jewish religiously-oriented mind with the greatest impact.

It is said that the Jewish council felt that Jesus **deserved** death. The Sanhedrin could not make such a sentence (John 18:31), and it is unlikely that the Romans would have given them such power. It is therefore likely that the council served

⁶⁵ And some began to spit on him, and to cover his face, and to strike him, saying to him, "Prophesy!" and the guards received him with blows.

⁶⁶ And as Peter was below in the courtyard, one of the maids of the high priest came; ⁶⁷ and seeing Peter warming himself, she looked at him, and said, "You also were with the Nazarene, Jesus." ⁶⁸ But he denied it, saying, "I neither know nor understand what you mean." And he went out into the gateway. ᶠ ⁶⁹ And the maid saw him, and began again to say to the bystanders, "This man is one of them." ⁷⁰ But again he denied it. And after a little while again the bystanders said to Peter, "Certainly you are one of them; for you are a Galilean." ⁷¹ But he began to invoke a curse on himself and to swear, "I do not know this man of whom you speak."

ᶠ Or *fore-court*. Other ancient authorities add *and the cock crowed*

---

only as a sort of grand jury. In the Roman judicial system there was no public prosecutor, and the governor might have used the council in bringing charges. This would mean that the Sanhedrin was not functioning as a court according to the requirements recorded in the Mishna. Hence, the problems that are usually brought up in connection with Jesus' trial before them (night meeting, non-agreement of witnesses, sentencing on the same day, etc.) are irrelevant.

[65] The implication that Jesus was blindfolded and could not see is explicitly stated in Luke 22:64. They **began to spit** on Jesus and the mocking included the challenge for Jesus to **prophesy,** that is, identify those who had done the spitting. It is profitable to ponder the scene devotionally from two aspects, the utter humiliation of Jesus and the depravity of his tormentors. It is difficult to conceive the Lord of the Christian confession ever having been so abused. Yet, it is no less a problem to understand the forces that created the mentality that would stoop to treat any human being as this one was treated.

[66-72] The account of the preliminary hearing was concluded in the incident of Peter's denial, surely the lowest point in Peter's relationship with Jesus (that all this was necessary, see comments on vs. 31). Mark's reader has been well prepared. Jesus has clearly stated that both a general

[72] And immediately the cock crowed a second time. And Peter remembered how Jesus had said to him, "Before the cock crows twice, you will deny me three times." And he broke down and wept.

[1] And as soon as it was morning the chief priests, with the elders and scribes, and the whole council held a consultation; and they bound Jesus and led him away and delivered him to Pilate. [2] And Pilate asked him, "Are you the King of the Jews?" And he answered him, "You have said so." [3] And the chief priests accused him of many things. [4] And Pilate again asked him, "Have you no answer to make? See how many charges they bring against you." [5] But Jesus made no further answer, so that Pilate wondered.

(the disciples) and a specific (Peter) denial would occur (vss. 26-31). And, further, Peter has been placed at the scene (vs. 54).

Peter made three separate denials, two in reaction to one of the **maids of the high priest,** and one to the **bystanders.** The implication seems to be that the maid thought she had seen Peter in a company with Jesus. The accusation of the bystanders was based upon their conclusion that he was a Galilean, because his accent betrayed him (Matt. 26:73). To this point, everything in the story seems so earthly. But then the sound of the cock was heard and to Peter it was little less than the voice of the Lord. Luke comments, "the Lord turned and looked at Peter."

Peter **broke down and wept.** It should not be forgotten that there were two who denied Jesus in a dramatic way that fateful night, Judas and Peter. Of the two, Peter's reaction—although surely painful—was a thousand times more productive. It is quite clear in the larger context that a man was being prepared to defend the risen Lord, and rather than denying Jesus before servants, Peter was soon ready to take his defense to some of the highest authorities in the land (see esp. Acts 3, 4).

The Trial before Pilate, 15:1-15 (Matt. 27:1-26; Luke 23:1-5, 17-28)

[1-5] The **consultation** of the **council** formalized Jesus'

⁶Now at the feast he used to release for them one prisoner for whom they asked. ⁷And among the rebels in prison, who had committed murder in the insurrection, there was a man called Barabbas. ⁸And the crowd came up and began to ask Pilate to do as he was wont to do for them. ⁹And he answered them, "Do you want me to release for you the King of the Jews?" ¹⁰For he perceived that it was out of envy that the chief priests had delivered him up. ¹¹But the chief priests stirred up the crowd to have him release for them Barabbas instead.

---

condemnation on the part of the Jews. To this point in the proceedings they exercised what may seem to many considerable freedom to see to their own affairs. This of course was the nature of the famous *pax Romana*. The Jews could not, however, execute anyone without Roman approval, indeed, effecting the execution "by the hand of lawless men" (see comments on 14:63, 64). As the Romans would not recognize any religious "crime" as grounds for such action, the Jews felt it necessary to make Jesus at least appear to be a threat to the Roman political establishment. The accusation therefore was **the King of the Jews.** Jesus' reply is quite correctly translated. **You have said so.** It would appear that this statement should be understood as a rather ambiguous affirmative. It is certainly not negative; yet, it is not strongly affirmative. Why did Jesus feel the need to be ambiguous at this point, especially in the light of his strong affirmative answer to the high priest earlier (14:62)? The answer is simple. Jesus rejected Pilate's definition of terms (for what "Christ" meant to Pilate, see 15:12, 18, 26, 29, 32). Jesus did not accept Pilate's understanding; therefore, he answered ambiguously. The charges grow (15:3ff.).

[6-10] It was customary for the Romans to release a prisoner **at the feast** as a sort of good-will gesture toward the Jews. At this particular feast there was one, Barabbas, in prison who seemed to many to be the most likely prospect. Pilate thought otherwise. He felt that this would be a good opportunity to effect the release of Jesus. He had this desire because **he perceived that it was out of envy that the chief priests had delivered him up.**

[11-13] The chief priest began to stir up the crowd. They could not resist Pilate's judgment by themselves. Pilate

¹² And Pilate again said to them, "Then what shall I do with the man whom you call the King of the Jews?" ¹³ And they cried out again, "Crucify him." ¹⁴ And Pilate said to them "Why, what evil has he done?" But they shouted all the more, "Crucify him." ¹⁵ So Pilate, wishing to satisfy the crowd, released for them Barabbas; and having scourged Jesus, he delivered him to be crucified.

¹⁶ And the soldiers led him away inside the palace (that is, the praetorium); and they called together the whole battalion. ¹⁷ And they clothed him in a purple cloak, and plaiting a crown of thorns they put it on him. ¹⁸ And they began to salute him, "Hail, King of the Jews!" ¹⁹ And they struck his head with a reed, and spat upon him, and they knelt down in homage to him. ²⁰ And when they had mocked him, they stripped him of the purple cloak, and put his own clothes on him. And they led him out to crucify him.

---

apparently thought at this point that just to ask what to **do** with Jesus would begin to put things right. How wrong he was! The crowd, now actively involved in what was happening, replied, **Crucify him!**

[14, 15] Pilate made his third and last attempt to do what was right with Jesus. He inquired as to what **evil** he had done. There was no real answer. In fact, in the midst of such confusion it is difficult even to imagine the question. The cry of the mob persisted, **Crucify him.** Pilate, wishing to satisfy the crowd, gave in to their desire.

Pilate's attempt to do what was right with Jesus should be viewed as reasonably honorable. He was wrong, even by his own Roman standards. That much is clear. Yet, it must be remembered that Roman control in Jerusalem was always somewhat questionable (cf. Lysias, Acts 23:12-35; cf. comments on 14:1, 2). If Pilate understood Jesus to be just another Jew, this was not too high a price to pay even for temporary peace in the city. If he had taken a determined course with respect to the cause of justice, there was a good chance that a number of people might be killed, including Pilate himself.

The Mocking, 15:16-20 (Matt. 27:27-31)

[16-20] The details of this incident need little clarifica-

181

²¹ **And they compelled a passer-by, Simon of Cyrene, who was coming in from the country, the father of Alexander and Rufus, to carry his cross.** ²² **And they brought him to the place called Golgotha (which means the place of a skull).** ²³ **And they offered him wine mingled with myrrh; but he did not take it.**

---

tion. On the basis of an assumption which they may or may not have regarded as true, the Roman soldiers were permitted mockingly to dress Jesus as a king and "to have themselves a little fun." The purpose of the incident may have been to produce a mood in the soldiers themselves that would enable them to execute Jesus.

The humiliation must be regarded as the most distasteful feature. Serious reflection makes it possible to see the impossibility of description. In fact, for any disciple—then or now —to think seriously about the way in which Jesus was treated here is to react with the greatest repugnance.

The Road to Golgotha, 15:21-32 (Matt. 27:32-44; Luke 23:26-43)

Once the soldiers had completed their mockery, the machinery to effect the crucifixion was set in motion. Many more or less "innocent" people—including the soldiers— were about to participate in an act the effects of which would be among the most far-reaching in the history of man. Yet, little did they know.

[21] In spite of the dastardly thing being done to Jesus, there is an apparent humanity that appears occasionally in the narrative. Here it is in the form of someone to help Jesus carry his cross. Mark describes **Simon of Cyrene** as **the father of Alexander and Rufus,** a phrase which is omitted in the parallel passages. One "Rufus" is mentioned in Romans as "eminent in the Lord" and who had at least a metaphorical maternal connection with Paul (Rom. 16:13). If the two references do in fact allude to the same person, then here is some support for the statement that Mark's Gospel was produced "in the region of Italy."

[22, 23] **Wine** and **myrrh**, offered under circumstances such as these, were for the basic purpose of making the pain easier to bear. Once again a humanitarian act seems

182

²⁴ **And they crucified him, and divided his garments among them, casting lots for them, to decide what each should take.** ²⁵ **And it was the third hour, when they crucified him.** ²⁶ **And the inscription of the charge against him read, "The King of the Jews."** ²⁷ **And with him they crucified two robbers, one on his right and one on his left.**ᵍ ²⁹ **And those who passed by derided him, wagging their heads, and saying, "Aha! You who would destroy the temple and build it in three days,**

ᵍ Other ancient authorities insert verse 28, *And the scripture was fulfilled which says,* *"He was reckoned with the transgressors"*

---

momentarily to soften the extreme severity of the situation. The fact that Jesus refused to take it must be an indication of his determination to bear the total pain of the situation in order to accomplish the redemption of man. On the seamless robe see Psalm 22:18 and John 19:23, 24.

[24, 25] The act of **dividing his garments** must be allowed to speak of the nature of the circumstances. First it indicates the casualness with which some were able to react to the larger scene. And it stands as an estimate—at least by some —as to what might be made of this particular crucifixion. To put it in modern terms, consider the contrast in the value of a few pieces of second-hand clothing and spiritual "life."

[26] It is apparent throughout the various accounts of the crucifixion that the Romans were somewhat reluctant partners in the awful deed. If they could make any case for this Jesus being a threat to them politically, they could thereby ease their guilt in the situation. Therefore, they devised some sort of sign which claimed that this man was politically **the King of the Jews,** a farce begun by Herod shortly after Jesus' birth (see comments on 6:14ff.). And although the practice may have been regular, the implication here seems to be that the Romans were trying to make legitimate something inherently suspicious.

[27] Jesus was crucified between **two robbers.** At this point the improbability of the situation becomes overwhelming: first, a crucifixion for a **king,** but now a **king** between **two robbers.** Incredible! Some later texts follow Luke 22:37 in noting that it had been prophesied that Messiah would be "reckoned with transgressors."

[29-32] With Jesus nailed securely to the cross, some

[30] save yourself, and come down from the cross!" [31] So also the chief priests mocked him to one another with the scribes, saying, "He saved others; he cannot save himself. [32] Let the Christ, the King of Israel, come down from the cross, that we may see and believe." Those who were crucified with him also reviled him.

[33] And when the sixth hour had come, there was darkness over the whole land[h] until the ninth hour. [34] And at the ninth hour Jesus cried with a loud voice, "Eloi, Eloi, lama sabachthani?" which means, "My God, my God, why hast thou forsaken me?" [35] And some of the bystanders hearing it said, "Behold, he is calling Elijah." [36] And one ran and, filling a sponge full of vinegar, put it on a reed and gave it to him to drink, saying, "Wait, let us see whether Elijah will come to take him down." [37] And Jesus uttered a loud cry, and breathed his last.

[h] Or earth

---

of those who passed by became more open and flagrant in their denunciation. This can only be regarded as the expected reaction of the group, essentially the same as the mob earlier in their desire to have Jesus killed. Perhaps encouraged by the common people the **chief priests** joined in. So momentarily popular was this abuse, seemingly based upon Jesus' apparent lack of power to do anything about it, that even the robbers joined in the derision (however, cf. Luke 25:39ff.). Again, when one seriously contemplates the description of the scene, it becomes difficult to perceive how it all came to be so in the first place.

The Death on the Cross, 15:33-41 (Matt. 27:45-56; Luke 23: 44-49)

[33-37] At midday there was a change in the cir- cumstances surrounding the crucifixion. The three hours of agony which Jesus had endured in the morning were followed by three hours of darkness in the afternoon. Little is said explicitly about Jesus during this period. The emphasis seems to shift to the ominousness of the total scene. In the main, one is left to wonder what the average inhabitant of Jerusalem might have thought about such strange events.

³⁸ **And the curtain of the temple was torn in two, from top
to bottom.** ³⁹ **And when the centurion, who stood facing him,
saw that he thusⁱ breathed his last, he said, ''Truly this man
was the Son^x of God!''**

> ⁱ Other ancient authorities insert *cried out and*
> ^x Or *a son*

Matthew mentions that there were resurrections, but even
here one must imagine what their effect might have been.

Near the end of the period of darkness Jesus **cried** out,
''Eloi, Eloi, lama sabachthani?'' It is not without significance
that the Aramaic is included in the Greek (even the English)
text. Surely it must be concluded that Jesus spoke in the
language most familiar to him when he was under such severe
stress. In any case, his cry was misunderstood by the **bystanders.** They thought that he was attempting to call **Elijah.**
This is of course a reasonable misunderstanding when considering the basic sound involved, not to speak of the role
Elijah-speculation had played in Jewish thinking with regard
to Messiah (see comments on 6:15; 8:28). The **vinegar** is
to be understood as an attempt to relieve the pain. Perhaps
they thought that Jesus might say more. Further, they were
keen to see if perchance Elijah might in fact appear. Jesus
breathed his last.

[38] Abruptly, and for only a single verse, the scene
moves from a hill outside the city to the inside of the **Temple,**
indeed, to the partition within the Temple which separated
the main portion of the structure into two parts. This
division was patterned after a similar one in the wilderness
tabernacle. In the original circumstances, all priests could
enter the ''holy place'' but only the high priest could enter
the ''most holy place,'' and that only once each year.
Symbolically the ''holy place'' is likened to heaven where
the high priest (Christ) must penetrate the curtain (death),
in order that his disciples might follow. The tearing of the
Temple curtain was symbolic of the fact that the Servant had
suffered and that the significance and finality of death has
been removed. (A far-reaching symbolism of course, but
one which the writer of Hebrews develops fully.)

[39-41] At this point the centurion who watched Jesus
as he **breathed his last** made a remarkable statement which

⁴⁰ There were also women looking on from afar, among whom were Mary Magdalene, and Mary the mother of James the younger and of Joses, and Salome, ⁴¹ who, when he was in Galilee, followed him, and ministered to him; and also many other women who came up with him to Jerusalem.

⁴² And when evening had come, since it was the day of Preparation, that is, the day before the sabbath, ⁴³ Joseph of Arimathea, a respected member of the council, who was also himself looking for the kingdom of God, took courage and went to Pilate, and asked for the body of Jesus.

---

has been the point of scholarly interest for many years. He said, **Truly this man was the Son of God.** The fact that the definite article is missing in the Greek text results in the fact that a more accurate translation might be "a son of God," or perhaps even "a son of a god." No doubt the centurion was thinking in terms of his Roman background and not in revised Jewish messianic terms. But, for Mark, whether knowingly or not, the truth had been verbalized. This is the important thing; the purpose stated in Mark 1:1 was here made complete. One must therefore observe that "King of the Jews" (vss. 9, 12, 18, 26) and "the Christ the King of Israel" (vs. 32) may also be understood as unwitting proclamations of truth. The description of the scene is closed with a reference to some of the **women** who had followed Jesus from **Galilee** all the way to his crucifixion in **Jerusalem.**

The Burial of Jesus, 15:42-47 (Matt. 27:57-61: Luke 23:50-56)

[42, 43] The phrase **day of Preparation** *(paraskeuē)* was terminology used of the day preceding either a sabbath or a festival. There was much to be done on these days as the law (and the tradition) contained strict injuctions which severely limited physical activity on the sabbath itself. If anything were to be done with the body of Jesus, it had to be done immediately. After sundown no law-abiding Jew could take any further action. At this point **Joseph of Arimathea** entered the picture. He is described as a **respected** or honored **member of the council,** the Sanhedrin, which was the highest Jewish authority. Further, he **was also himself looking for the kingdom of God.** Whether Joseph was sympathetic with

186

44 And Pilate wondered if he were already dead; and
summoning the centurion, he asked him whether he was
already dead.[j] 45 And when he learned from the centurion
that he was dead, he granted the body to Joseph. 46 And he
bought a linen shroud, and taking him down, wrapped him in
the linen shroud, and laid him in a tomb which had been hewn
out of the rock; and he rolled a stone against the door of the
tomb. 47 Mary Magdalene and Mary the mother of Joses saw
where he was laid.

1 And when the sabbath was past, Mary Magdalene, and
Mary the mother of James, and Salome, bought spices, so
that they might go and anoint him. 2 And very early on the
first day of the week they went to the tomb when the sun
had risen.

[j] Other ancient authorities read *whether he had been some time dead*

---

the teaching of Jesus must remain obscure. He was **looking.** The text does not say whether he saw in Jesus that for which he was searching. Bodies of criminals were usually denied proper burial, so it follows that it was a courageous act for Joseph to go to **Pilate** and make the request he did.

[44-47] Pilate was apparently surprised that Joseph's request came as quickly as it did. Death by crucifixion usually took a longer period of time. If there were no severe loss of blood, it was not uncommon for a man to hang on his cross several days before expiring. When the **centurion** verified that Jesus was in fact dead, Pilate **granted the body to Joseph.** When Joseph had placed the body in a **linen shroud,** he put in in his own tomb. Both Matthew and Luke make a point of the tomb being new or unused. As it was not uncommon for tombs of the area and time to contain several burial places, presumably this is to imply that the resurrected individual could be none other than this particular man. The disk shaped **stone** was primarily designed to protect the body from vandals or even certain animals. Again, a peculiar note is sounded in the closing line of the paragraph, which records that some of the women were looking on.

The Empty Tomb, 16:1-8 (Mark 28:1-10; Luke 24:1-11)

[1, 2] Apparently those closest to Jesus made it their business to observe carefully the laws and traditions con-

³ And they were saying to one another, "Who will roll away the stone for us from the door of the tomb?" ⁴ And looking up, they saw that the stone was rolled back—it was very large. ⁵ And entering the tomb, they saw a young man sitting on the right side, dressed in a white robe; and they were amazed. ⁶ And he said to them, "Do not be amazed; you seek Jesus of Nazareth, who was crucified. He has risen, he is not here; see the place where they laid him.

cerning the sabbath. There is, however, the feeling embedded in this text that they were anxious for this particular sabbath to pass so they could further express their love and devotion to their crucified leader. The phrase when the sabbath was past could open the possiblity that this incident occurred shortly after sundown on Saturday. Some have seen something of a contradiction between this phrase and the later one, early on the first day of the week. The passage as a unit seems to leave little doubt, however, that Mark intended his readers to understand the daylight portion of the day after the sabbath.

[3, 4] The stone that had been placed over the opening to the tomb was very large and therefore presented a problem to them in their desire to anoint the body of Jesus. Although they had this problem, they did not feel it was insurmountable. They had no plan; they simply discussed the problem of getting it removed. Their attitude in this seems remarkable. Although they knew that of themselves they could not move the stone, they made elaborate preparations in full confidence that somehow they would solve the problem. When they arrived they were surprised to find the tomb already open.

[5, 6] They entered the tomb and were somewhat amazed to see a young man *(neaniskon)* sitting on the right side (a phrase which underscores the basic historical feeling contained in the passage). There can be little doubt that this is to be understood as an angelic being (see Matt. 28:2, 5; Luke 24:4, 23; John 20:12). The young man calmed the women and anticipated the purpose of their presence: you seek Jesus of Nazareth. Then the angelic being made two unequivocal statements: He has risen, he is not here. This must be understood as a dramatic way of pointing at the

[7]But go, tell his disciples and Peter that he is going before you
to Galilee; there you will see him, as he told you." [8]And they
went out and fled from the tomb; for trembling and astonishment had come upon them; and they said nothing to anyone,
for they were afraid.

---

fact that "though we once regarded Christ from a human
point of view, we regard him thus no longer" (2 Cor. 5:16).

[7] The women were given clear and concise instructions
to inform Jesus' **disciples and Peter** of the situation. Perhaps
Peter is mentioned specifically because he had come
to hold, and was to continue to occupy, a place of great
importance among them. Then there is the reference to the
fact that the appearances were to occur in Galilee as they
had been told. This may be a way to honor the fact that
these women had come from **Galilee,** although there is a
Galilean emphasis in Mark that has led scholars in more
recent times to observe that at the approximate
date of the writing of the Gospel (see Introduction), that
is, during and after the destruction of Jerusalem, many
Palestinian Christians had gathered at Pella in Galilee. Such
a hypothesis merits some attention.

[8] At least temporarily, the women did just the opposite
of what they had been told: **They . . . fled . . . for trembling
and astonishment had come upon them.** Surely one must
grant a little time for human minds to absorb the events
which they had experienced. It is not without significance
that women, who were severely regarded in that time and
place, were allowed to play this leading role at this particular
point in the development of events. Thus Mark's Gospel,
in the ending of the best manuscripts, closes on the note
of fear struck in the hearts of these women as they attempted
to take in these marvelous events. Such a reaction is not
without significance. Fear here is a holy fear, the fear in
presence of revelation, and is sometimes associated with
faith (4:35-41; 5:33, 36). This fear in Mark is more intense
than "amazement." The latter has more to do with responses
to reports about Jesus (1:27; 5:20; 6:2, 6; 7:37; 10:24, 26,
etc.) whereas fear appears as a direct response to the divine
act. It regularly marks the initial recognition that God had

189

⁹ Now when he rose early on the first day of the week, he appeared first to Mary Magdalene, from whom he had cast out seven demons. ¹⁰ She went and told those who had been with him, as they mourned and wept. ¹¹ But when they heard that he was alive and had been seen by her, they would not believe it.

---

acted and the expectation implied is that it should result in faith. Before Caesarea Philippi (8:27ff.) fear occurred in response to acts of messianic power. Afterward, it was the passion prediction which caused fear (9:32; 10:32).

EPILOGUE, 16:9-20

Resurrection Appearances, 16:9-18

The textual evidence seems to support the view that verses 9-20 were not the original ending of the Gospel. Nothing is actually lost in this view as everything contained in these verses is documented elsewhere (for instance on vss. 9-11, cf. John 20:11-18; on vss. 12, 13, cf. Luke 24:13-35; on vss. 14-16, cf. Matt. 28:16-20 and Luke 24:36-49; on vss. 17-20, see the references in the notes below). The long ending is however attested as early as A.D. 150; if it is an addition, it was quite early and obviously reflects genuine information. Although some have argued that verse 8 was the intended conclusion of Mark's Gospel, this seems unlikely. No resurrection appearances are detailed in the short ending, but two references (14:28 and 16:8) point to them and lead one to expect them to be recorded. One seems to be left with the alternative that either the Gospel was for some unknown reason never finished, or its original ending was lost at a very early date.

[9-11] There are three different resurrection appearances recorded in these concluding verses. The first of these is to Mary Magdalene. In this connection it is admittedly strange that she is introduced as though the reader had not encountered her earlier—from whom he had cast out seven demons (see Luke 8:2). The stress in the first two incidents in the epilogue and the corrective purpose of the third is directed at the reluctance of the disciples to believe the

¹² **After this he appeared in another form to two of them, as they were walking into the country. ¹³ And they went back and told the rest, but they did not believe them.**

¹⁴ **Afterward he appeared to the eleven themselves as they sat at table; and he upbraided them for their unbelief and hardness of heart, because they had not believed those who saw him after he had risen. ¹⁵ And he said to them, "Go into all the world and preach the gospel to the whole creation. ¹⁶ He who believes and is baptized will be saved; but he who does not believe will be condemned.**

---

news of the resurrection. No doubt! One is left completely disoriented when trying to imagine what it might be like to encounter a friend whom one had seen die!

[12, 13] Recorded here in the briefest terms is a story famous for its clarity and detail in the third Gospel (Luke 24:36-49). Again the emphasis is placed upon the incredulity of the disciples. They were extremely reluctant to accept what their senses were saying had in fact happened. Luke says that they "disbelieved for joy." That is, they were overwhelmed with joy that Jesus—apparently at least—was alive, but they were having great difficulty accepting it. The reference to **another form** may say something about Jesus' ability to change in this new set of circumstances.

[14-16] Since lack of understanding and belief had become a common fault among the disciples, Jesus moved to do something about it. In an appearance to **the eleven** he forced the issue. They would have found it impossible not to accept his real physical presence. Nothing is said about the development of understanding within these disciples at this point but change there must have been. With the reality of the resurrection as a part of their being, all that was needed was the Holy Spirit to send the apostles on their way (Acts 2). Given the time and place, the commission to all the world can only be known from later New Testament documents, the subsequent execution of that commission was nothing short of wonderous. In the same connection, but in a different vein, there can be no doubt that belief and baptism were prerequisites not only to salvation but entrance into a new community as well.

191

¹⁷ And these signs will accompany those who believe: in my name they will cast out demons; they will speak in new tongues; ¹⁸ they will pick up serpents, and if they drink any deadly thing, it will not hurt them: they will lay their hands on the sick, and they will recover.''

¹⁹ So then the Lord Jesus, after he had spoken to them, was taken up into heaven, and sat down at the right hand of God. ²⁰ And they went forth and preached everywhere, while the Lord worked with them and confirmed the message by the signs that attended it. Amen.ᵏ

ᵏ Some of the most ancient authorities bring the book to a close at the end of verse 8. One authority concludes the book by adding after verse 8 the following: *But they reported briefly to Peter and those with him all that they had been told. And after this, Jesus himself sent out by means of them, from east to west, the sacred and imperishable proclamation of eternal salvation.* Other authorities include the preceding passage and continue with verses 9-20. In most authorities verses 9-20 follow immediately after verse 8; a few authorities insert additional material after verse 14.

[17, 18] Assurance is given in this context that these signs of confirmation did take place (see vs. 20), but detailed evidence from the later lives of the apostles is abundant also: (1) **cast out demons** (Acts 8:7; 16:18; 19:12); (2) **speak in new tongues** (Acts 2:4, 11, etc.; 10:46; 19:6; 1 Cor. 12:10, 28; 14:2ff.); (3) **pick up serpents** (Acts 28:3-6); (4) **lay hands on the sick** (Acts 28:8; cf. 3:7; 9:41). The only item not exampled is **drink any deadly thing.** It is interesting to note that this specific is mentioned conditionally. That is, **if** they should do this, no harm would follow.

Conclusion, 16:19 (cf. Luke 24:50-53; Heb. 2:4)

[19, 20] The Gospel epilogue concludes with a matter-of-fact statement concerning the ascension of the resurrected Jesus. In contrast with the Acts account (see chapter 1), no mention is made of any reaction on the part of the disciples. At any rate, the gospel story is closed with the account of yet another marvelous event. Jesus' followers **went** and **preached.** The good news was not so much defended as it was proclaimed. Subsequently, as far as these men were concerned, these things *had happened,* and they understood it to be their mandate to let all the world know about it.

192